*"Imagination grows by exercise, and contrary
to common belief, is more powerful in the
mature than in the young."*

W. Somerset Maugham

Develop Your Creative Skills

TIME
LIFE
BOOKS

Other Publications:
WEIGHT WATCHERS® SMART CHOICE RECIPE COLLECTION
THE AMERICAN INDIANS
LOST CIVILIZATIONS
CREATIVE EVERYDAY COOKING
THE ART OF WOODWORKING
TIME-LIFE LIBRARY OF CURIOUS AND UNUSUAL FACTS
HEALTHY HOME COOKING
HOME REPAIR AND IMPROVEMENT
ECHOES OF GLORY
AMERICAN COUNTRY
VOYAGE THROUGH THE UNIVERSE
MYSTERIES OF THE UNKNOWN
UNDERSTANDING COMPUTERS
FIX IT YOURSELF
COUNTRY LIFESTYLES
THE CIVIL WAR
THE ENCHANTED WORLD
TIME FRAME
WINGS OF WAR

For information on and a full description of any of the
Time-Life Books series listed above, please call
1-800-621-7026 weekdays between 9:00 a.m. and 6:00 p.m.
Eastern Standard Time, or write:
Reader Information
Time-Life Customer Service
P.O. Box C-32068
Richmond, Virginia 23261-2068

MINDPOWER

Develop Your Creative Skills

TIME-LIFE BOOKS
Alexandria, Virginia

MINDPOWER
Created, edited, and designed by DK Direct Limited,
23-24 Henrietta Street, London WC2E 8NA

A DORLING KINDERSLEY BOOK

DK DIRECT LIMITED

Series Editor Reg Grant
Deputy Series Editor Francis Ritter
Senior Editor Nina Hathway
Editors Edda Bohnsack, Rhoda Nottridge
Editorial Research Julie Whitaker

Series Art Editor Ruth Shane
Designers Amanda Carroll, Francis Cawley,
Christian Nouyou, Helen Spencer, John Strange
Picture Research Julia Tacey

Editorial Director Jonathan Reed; **Design Director** Ed Day
Production Manager Ian Paton

Series Consultant Dr. Glenn Wilson
Volume Consultant Dr. Robert L. Solso
Contributors Adrian Brewer, Peter Brookesmith, Dr. Howard E. Gruber,
Dr. Marcia Harrington, Dr. Thomas Harrington, Dr. Marvin Levine,
Dr. Robert L. Solso, Dr. Glenn Wilson

TIME-LIFE BOOKS

President John Hall
Editor-in-Chief Thomas H. Flaherty
Director of Editorial Resources Elise D. Ritter-Clough
Executive Art Director Ellen Robling

Editorial Director Lee Hassig
Marketing Director Regina Hall
Director of Production Services Robert N. Carr
Production Manager Marlene Zack

Time-Life Books staff for Develop Your Creative Skills

Editorial Director Robert Doyle
Associate Editor/Research-Writing Daniel Kulpinski
Series Consultant Richard M. Restak, M.D.

Time-Life Books is a division of Time-Life Inc.,
a wholly owned subsidiary of THE TIME INC. BOOK COMPANY

Library of Congress Cataloging in Publication Data

Develop your creative skills.
p.   cm. — (Mindpower ; v. 3)
"A Dorling Kindersley book" — T.p. verso.
Includes bibliographical references and index.
ISBN 0-7835-1262-7 (hard)
1. Creative ability   I. Time-Life Books.   II. Series.
BF408.D487   1993
153.3'5—dc20   93-6914

CONTENTS

INTRODUCTION

NOT LONG AGO, CREATIVITY was a word seldom heard outside artistic circles; it was a term reserved for solitary geniuses. But today, flexibility and originality are prized in many professions, from scientific research and engineering to personnel management. Creativity can also play a significant part in everyday living. Devising a fresh and useful solution, even for a small problem, is a satisfying exercise in creativity. Once you let creativity flourish, it can increase your personal fulfillment in all aspects of life—from household repairs and cooking to conversation and relationships.

Of course, writing a symphony or painting a picture is generally viewed as a more creative activity than inventing a fresh marketing strategy or a new recipe. But as psychologist Abraham Maslow wrote, "It is better to make a first-class soup than a second-rate painting." One big difference between an artist in front of a blank canvas and, say, an engineer designing a bridge is that when they are finished, the painter's work will be much harder to evaluate.

Personal flair

While some endeavors call for more invention than others, virtually any activity can be more rewarding if approached with a measure of creativity. Preparing a meal for guests is a practical example. Many home cooks are skilled at producing tempting dinners. Following detailed recipes, they assemble, measure, and combine ingredients, planning and coordinating their preparations so that all the hot dishes are ready at the same moment. Carrying out this complex process with care and attention calls for many valuable skills, but not for creativity.

True creativity shows itself in that extra personal flair that some people add to their activities. Above all, it reveals itself in the production of something new—an unusual twist to a recipe or a new way of presenting a dish. If, for example, you replace anchovies with capers in your favorite pasta sauce, acting on an intuitive feeling that this will work, then you are cooking creatively. If you take on a recipe as only the roughest of guides, if you improvise variants and invent surprising combinations of foods, and still serve crowd-pleasing meals, then you are a very creative cook indeed.

Creativity should not be confused with lack of discipline, carelessness, or novelty for its own sake. If you sit at a piano and hit the keyboard at random, you may make a sequence of notes that has never been heard before. But you are not being

---

Dare to take flight
The art of leading a more creative life depends partly on learning to see the world in a new light. The first step is to practice freeing your mind from fixed ways of thinking.

WAYS WITH WORDS

Stimulate your mind with this test of verbal flexibility and fluency. Based on discovering synonyms—different words that have the same meaning—the test requires you to look at a single word from a variety of angles, jumping from one context to another.

For example, "sweet" can mean kind (a generous act), sugary (taste), cute (a baby), pretty (a face), melodious (a tune), and pleasurable (an experience).

SWEET

KIND

SUGARY

CUTE

For each of the six words below, try to think up at least six different synonyms:

HOT	YOUNG
SOFT	COOL
SIMPLE	TOUGH

When you have completed your lists, compare them with the suggestions on page 134.

any more creative than a cat scampering up and down the keys. The path to creativity often meanders through the strange and impractical, but in the end it must lead to a product or performance that fulfills a purpose admirably. As writer Mark Twain once observed, "The man with a new idea is a crank until the idea succeeds."

Develop originality

In recent decades, experts have come to believe that anybody can learn to think and act in fresh, original, and, consequently, more productive ways. This volume will explain how creativity works and offer a variety of techniques and exercises aimed at developing your creative talents.

Start right away by limbering up on the tests on these pages and the two that follow on pages 10 and 11; these are designed to stimulate your mind to think more creatively. You may wish to do them with a friend so you can encourage each other and compare results. These puzzles will give you a feel for the style, the fun, and the sheer challenge of creative thinking.

Creativity is intrinsically hard to measure, because it involves producing novel ideas or solutions that cannot be assessed simply as "right" or "wrong." For this reason, these tests, and those you will find in the rest of the volume, do not generally yield a clear score that places you high or low on a creativity scale. Rather, they invite you to reflect on your own performance and to consider the strengths and the weaknesses of your current abilities.

See through the myths

Perhaps because its sources are hidden in the invisible wellsprings of personality and the mysterious recesses of the brain, creativity itself has been shrouded in myths and misconceptions. Chapter 1 separates the facts from fancy. Much has been made, for example, of the brain's two hemispheres. Some people believe that creativity depends on "right-brained thinking." While it is true that each side of the brain has its own specialities, the notion that one side of the head is superior to the other— that only one side does the inspired work—doesn't hold up. Recent studies suggest quite the opposite in fact, revealing that the key to creative thought lies in productive collaboration between the right and left hemispheres of the brain.

Equally misunderstood are geniuses, people with outstanding creative powers. These exceptional individuals are often held in awe, and regarded as near-magical beings who are set apart from the rest of humanity. But inventor Thomas Edison got it right when he defined genius as "one percent inspiration, 99 percent perspiration." On the whole, geniuses get their highly creative results by working much harder than other people.

Apart from the hard work and perseverance that are so crucial to creative success, probably the single trait that most distinguishes creative people is originality. Confronted with a problem in any area of their life—at work or at home—creative people

MEET YOUR MATCH

You may remember some of these matchstick tests from your schooldays, but they can still challenge your creativity.

For each test, from one to four, first lay out the matches as shown at right, then alter the patterns according to the instructions below. It is possible, though more difficult, to do the puzzles in your head.

Success depends on mentally freeing the matches from their original configuration. Turn to page 134 for the answers.

1. Form six equal triangles by moving four matches.

2. Form four squares by moving three matches. Then try to do it by only moving two.

3. Form four squares by taking away three matches.

4. Form four equilateral triangles using all six matches.

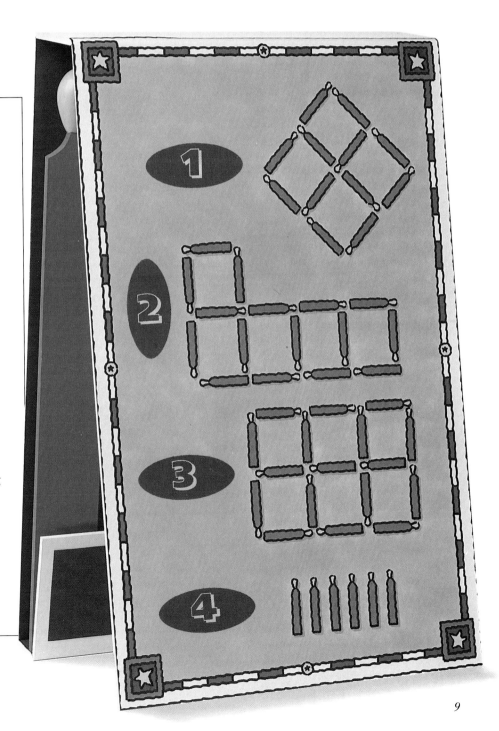

Brave new world
To liberate yourself from fixed ways of thinking, play the "what if" game. What if, for example, everyone had three legs instead of two—how would life be different? Shoes and trousers would cost more. Skiing might be easier, with a third leg for extra balance, but riding a horse or a bicycle could be problematic. Using the illustration for inspiration, see how many additional differences you can think of (some potential solutions are outlined on page 135).

will usually look for novel solutions that sidestep the familiar and well-trodden path.

The tendency of creative people to possess qualities such as perseverance and originality would seem to show that creativity is as much a matter of personality as it is of acquiring specific skills. Although anyone can learn to be creative, some people find that it comes quite naturally. The first chapter of this volume ends with a questionnaire that will help you identify in yourself the traits associated with being creative. The results will help you focus on the aspects of your personality that would benefit from some attention.

The second chapter is devoted to developing creativity in problem solving. It examines new ways out of the mental ruts that lead to dead ends when original solutions are called for. You can learn a whole range of tricks and techniques for getting brand-new angles on apparently insoluble

problems. For example, try Edward de Bono's much-discussed lateral thinking, or pick words at random from a dictionary to stimulate a fresh train of thought. These, combined with many other techniques, will help you conquer a wide range of problems—everything from marketing difficulties to household appliances on the blink. You can learn to avoid the form of rigid thinking called problem blindness, and replace it with much more flexible patterns of thought.

Sustain the momentum

Naturally, solving problems isn't all there is to creativity. The third chapter in this volume, "The creative process," describes how to set about a sustained creative effort. The principles apply to any endeavor you might choose—whether you want to improve your photography, try your hand at writing fiction, or develop skills in a craft.

Creative techniques can transform casual dabbling in such areas into more exciting output. You can learn to look for inspiration instead of waiting for it to come to you, and find out how to overcome the occasional blocks that impede your progress. Another important step is to provide yourself with a stimulating environment.

Creativity, however, is not always a solo pursuit. Groups can be creative, too, and many modern companies in search of innovation are exploring ways to help employees team up productively. Chapter 4, "Group creativity," will help you evaluate your workplace as a spawning ground for fresh thinking, and show you how to use the oft-misunderstood technique of brainstorming. One group, using this method, came up with 89 ideas for reducing absenteeism in a single half-hour session. Group creativity may be even more powerful than the solitary variety, since it lets people pool their talents and compensate for one another's weaknesses. The key is in making sure that all participants are properly organized and motivated.

Developing your personal creativity is a lifelong pursuit. It can be nurtured at any age—childhood, adulthood, or retirement. The final chapter explains how to encourage and preserve originality in children while putting some childlike freshness into your own life. This section of the book offers help in deciding where creative energy might best be channeled. And it suggests a more original approach to your everyday life, from the presents you give to the way you decorate your home.

Set your mind free

The tests in this book are designed to encourage and challenge your creativity. Some of them may seem tough at first, but perseverance will be rewarded. Approach the exercises playfully: A sense of humor will work wonders in setting your originality free. And watch out for the internal "judge" that finds fault with new ideas and experiences. The more you succeed in ignoring such worries, the more you will gain.

Above all, do not be afraid of making mistakes. Albert Einstein, the Nobel prize-winning physicist, once wrote, "A person who never made a mistake, never tried anything new." The key to creative thinking is to learn to look at the world in a different way. And that should come rather easily by the time you reach the end of this volume.

Picture this

Develop your creative imagination by focusing your mind on the two pictures at left. Study them carefully, then make up as many different stories as you can for each, linking all the unusual, disparate elements in the illustrations, and explaining what is going on. For example, you might start by asking yourself what is in the satchel in the first picture, why there is a rose on the desk, and how the window got broken. Turn to page 135 for two sample stories.

CHAPTER ONE

IN SEARCH OF CREATIVITY

THE QUEST FOR creativity has taken people down some very strange pathways. At one time, the creative spirit was believed to be a gift from the gods, and over the centuries, many myths and mysteries grew up around it. People who possessed this gift were described as geniuses and treated as though they were surrounded by a sacred aura. Ordinary mortals sought their own inspiration through mind-altering drugs and meditation.

Psychologists now believe that all people possess some degree of creative potential, and—even better—that they can bring this power to fruition with the proper training.

This opening chapter will help you to take stock of the creative skills you already possess by showing you how flexible your thinking is, how fluently you can generate fresh ideas, and how original your mind can be. If you find that some of the tests in this section are difficult, remember that creativity is something that can be learned.

The chapter also looks at the personality characteristics associated with high creativity. Most creative people, for example, have a great tolerance for situations that are ambiguous or unclear. Far from being fazed by chaos, they rejoice in its potential for novelty and for generating new forms of order. After you have tested yourself for personality traits that are closely related to creativity, you can consider how to cultivate such characteristics.

Creativity is not just about writing the great American novel or pondering ways to reverse the greenhouse effect. It is a principle for everyday life. The more you enhance your creativity, the more you will enjoy your day-to-day routine, your work and your hobbies, and your relationships.

In the end, the surest way to get on the creative path is to concentrate on the things that are important to you and have confidence in your own abilities. Take your original insights seriously, work diligently on them, and make them work for you. From modest beginnings you can achieve great improvements—the potential for change is in your hands.

TAKE CENTER STAGE IN EXPLORING

THE POSSIBILITIES THAT LIE WITHIN YOU; OPEN YOUR MIND

TO NEW IDEAS AND FRESH APPROACHES.

WHAT IS CREATIVITY?

CREATIVITY IS A FRUSTRATINGLY elusive concept to pin down. It is "one of those things," British design historian Stephen Bayley once suggested, "that is much easier to detect than to define." Fortunately, you can invite, experience, develop, and enjoy creativity without ever having to define it precisely.

But an understanding of the mental processes involved can definitely help you tap into your own creative energy. Armed with a better idea of how it works, you can begin to develop and use this facility in ways that might never have occurred to you.

One early but insightful analysis of the way creativity operates was proposed in the 1920s. British sociologist Graham Wallas perceived the creative process as a sequence of four indispensable stages, which he called preparation, incubation, illumination, and verification.

1. Preparation: True creativity in any field can rest only on firm knowledge and understanding of that field. Before you can create something original in pottery, for instance, you must first know how to shape a lump of clay and fire the resulting form. Only after working with simple pots and gaining understanding of the materials can you bring original designs into being. You must build from the ground up.

While knowledge is a necessary foundation for creativity, however, it can become a barrier if it leads to what psychologists call "rule-dominant behavior." Someone who always follows established practices cannot consider new ways of doing things. A confident, inquisitive attitude toward the subject at hand is important.

2. Incubation: Wallas believed that although creative thought begins in the conscious mind, it must be left to incubate in the more flexible unconscious before it can reach its full potential. The best way to solve a problem, he claimed, is to formulate it as clearly as possible using your knowledge of the subject, consider the matter thoroughly, and then forget all about it for some period of time. This theory is borne out in everyday experience; it is often only when you have stopped concentrating on a problem that the solution reveals itself.

3. Illumination: In what is sometimes referred to as a "eureka!" experience (see page 34), the answer to a problem often comes to mind without warning. This is frequently accompanied by a feeling of certainty that the solution is correct.

4. Verification: However inspired an idea may be, it must be made practical and workable. One way of evaluating an original notion is to write it down, and then analyze it critically and repeatedly.

In Wallas's model of the creative-thinking process, everyone can accomplish the preparation stage by choosing some subject to learn about. Incubation and

An elusive quality
Sometimes fluid, creativity is more often
mercurial—it slips through your hands like
quicksilver, refusing to be limited or defined.

READ THE COLORS

Creative people need to think logically and verbally while simultaneously using more primitive mental processes. The Stroop Color Test measures your ability to exercise two skills at once—word recognition and color recognition.

Move down the list of nonsense words in column A as quickly as possible, simply naming the color of each word as you look at it. Then do the same for column B, again calling out the colors of the words as quickly as you can.

A	B
ZYP	RED
QKLEF	BLACK
SWURG	YELLOW
XCIDB	BLUE
WOPR	GREEN
SWURG	BLACK
XCIDB	BLUE
QKLEF	RED
WOPR	YELLOW
ZYP	BLACK
SWURG	GREEN
XCIDB	BLUE
QKLEF	RED
WOPR	YELLOW
ZYP	GREEN
XCIDP	BLACK

People almost invariably find it more difficult to perform this exercise for the right-hand column, because they are stymied by the conflict between the meaning of the words and the colors in which they are printed.

According to research, the more quickly and accurately you can call out the colors in column B, the more mentally flexible you are and therefore the more proficient you are likely to be at creative thinking. Even after practicing the test, however, almost everyone will experience some degree of conflict between the colors of the words and their meanings.

illumination, however, are more mysterious and elusive. He firmly believed, though, that people who had learned how to evaluate their creative output were well on the way to enhancing it.

A question of style

Another way to look at creative thought processes is to analyze different styles of thinking. One useful classification was suggested by psychologist Joy Paul Guilford in his pioneering work at the University of Southern California in the 1950s. Guilford identified two kinds of thinking, which he characterized as "divergent" and "convergent."

To understand the difference between these two thinking styles, consider the two possible ways of approaching a question such as, "How are a peach and a banana similar?" Convergent thinking involves logic and deductive reasoning, and leads to only one correct answer—they are both fruit. Divergent thinking, on the other hand, requires imagination, flexibility, and originality; it looks at each problem in several different ways and allows for a number of answers. If you apply divergent thinking to this example, you could reply that both bananas and peaches are perishable, they make good compost, they squash if you sit on them, they can be thrown at performing artists, and on and on ad infinitum. You can, no doubt, think of many such connections yourself.

You must recognize and nurture the ability to think divergently before you can develop true creativity. Convergent thinking is also important, however; it helps you to order and evaluate a mass of divergent ideas.

Since the 1950s, there has been a great deal of interest in developing tests to measure people's creative abilities, particularly as a method of assessing job applicants. Joy Paul Guilford developed a series of such tests, which he based on his concepts of divergent and convergent thinking.

The exercises on pages 20 to 23—all of which will help you to evaluate your creativity in using

TWO ORDERS OF CREATIVITY

You are playing chess with a friend when you suddenly discover a fresh line of attack. True, it is not something that is completely new to the world of chess—but for you it is an entirely original idea. English psychologist Margaret Boden calls this kind of problem solving "psychological creativity."

In her book *The Creative Mind*, Boden suggests that there are two kinds of creativity—psychological and historical. Everyone is capable of the original thinking needed to come up with ideas that they have never thought of before. They might, for example, discover a new route that shortens the drive to their workplace. Psychological creativity is relatively common, and can be achieved easily by everybody.

What Boden calls "historical creativity" produces ideas that are new to the whole of human history—Einstein's theory of relativity, for example. As you might expect, this kind of creativity is much rarer than the more personal variety.

words and images—have been adapted from the Guilford tests and from those of another American psychologist, E. Paul Torrance.

Torrance developed his tests in the 1960s chiefly for measuring creativity in schoolchildren. He identified the four most important factors in Guilford's tests and used them as a base on which to build his own evaluative system. The elements of creativity that Torrance focused on were fluency, flexibility, originality, and elaboration.

Keeping score

Tests for fluency pose an open-ended problem and measure the test taker's total number of ideas or responses. The measure of flexibility is the variety in the responses, since variety demonstrates that the thinker can switch quickly from one idea or realm of thought to another. Originality is scored for novel, subtle solutions, and elaboration is found in the richness and depth of detail in the responses.

Judging these qualities, however, is not simple. Guilford and Torrance both wrote manuals for scoring their tests, but their detailed guidance betrays the fact that objective measurement of creativity is a slippery goal. For tests of fluency or divergent thinking, scoring by simply counting the responses seems to work reasonably well. On the other hand, scoring tests of flexibility and originality requires judgment, and the opinions of the scorers can vary widely. Scoring becomes even more subjective when the tests are based on pictures rather than words.

Like-minded

One measure of creativity, according to tests devised by E. Paul Torrance, is the ability to think flexibly and fluently. Finding ways to link dissimilar objects exercises this ability. The more ways you can think of to make a link, the more you are thinking creatively. Here is an example: How many similarities are there between a snake and an apple? Some possible solutions include: A snake and an apple both bothered Adam and Eve in the Garden of Eden; both have skins; both have no limbs; both can be found in grass.

Some tests, although they do not measure creativity itself, measure aptitudes that creative people tend to possess. The bases for such correlations are neither obvious nor well-understood, but exercises such as the Stroop Color Test (on page 16) seem to be valid indicators of creativity. Equally revealing are puzzles that evaluate field independence—the ability to perceive images disguised in a complex background pattern; examples appear below and on the facing page. It seems that performing well at these exercises may involve the integrated use of different parts of the brain, and this ability to use the whole brain is a hallmark of creative people.

One way to check the validity of a creativity test of the Guilford or Torrance type is to try it on people whose creativity has been recognized. Unfortunately, few of these tests deliver the expected results; people who are recognized as creative do not always produce high scores.

Resistant to testing

The upshot is that many creative traits are—for the present at least—unmeasurable. Tests cannot register the productivity or persistence that a creative person brings to a task. Nor can they measure the ability to think independently or take risks, attitudes that are indispensable to creativity. Worst of all, since highly innovative people tend to be nonconformists, they might balk at being tested for creativity anyway.

Probably the most important single lesson to be learned from creativity testing is the ability to recognize creative ways of thinking. Such recognition may, in the long term, help to make you a more original thinker.

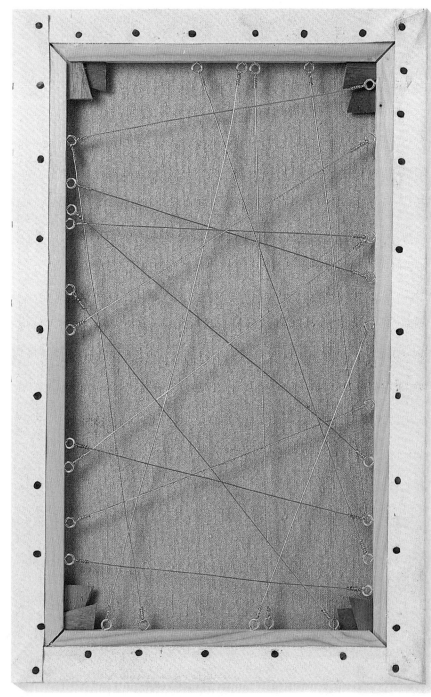

Star gazing
How many five-pointed star shapes can you see concealed in this intricate pattern of criss-crossed lines? An ability to make out hidden images in this way uses a skill that psychologists call field independence. People who possess this skill to a high degree may well display an aptitude for creative pursuits. The answer is on page 135.

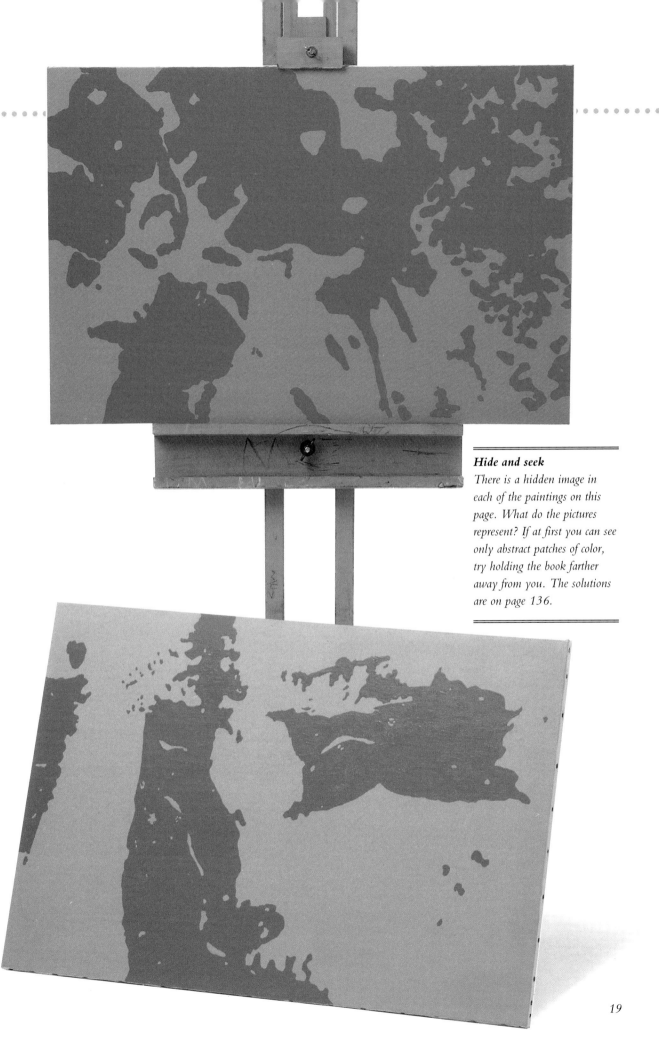

Hide and seek

There is a hidden image in each of the paintings on this page. What do the pictures represent? If at first you can see only abstract patches of color, try holding the book farther away from you. The solutions are on page 136.

19

MEASURE YOUR CREATIVITY

The following tests will help you measure your creativity. They are based on tests devised by a number of psychologists, among them J. P. Guilford and E. P. Torrance. You may find certain exercises harder than others, depending on which of your creative skills are already developed. When you look at the solutions suggested on pages 22 and 23, bear in mind that it is very difficult to measure creativity and that these tests can only attempt a rough assessment.

If you find the tests difficult, remember that you are only at the beginning of the book. There will be plenty of opportunity for you to practice and develop your creativity farther.

CREATIVE CONNECTIONS

This test measures the creative skills involved in finding connections between words that seem unrelated. Your task is to find a single word that links each group of three words given below. For example, the words "blood," "eye," and "light" can all be connected with the word "red" (blood red, red-eye, and red light). Limit yourself to 10 minutes for this test.

Turn to the solutions on page 22 to see how well you scored.

1. doll coat hold
2. horse spray shore
3. stool big ball
4. corn web nut
5. income return sales
6. wall key mason
7. hole hunt power
8. steeple up knife
9. turn all come
10. spot tan day

Letter lengtheners

This test exercises your ability to think fluently. Jot down a list of four-word phrases, using the four-letter sequence you are given to provide the first letter of each word. The aim is to produce as many phrases as possible; they must make some sense, however odd. For example, for the letters S I D E, the following phrases would be appropriate:

Said In Deadly Earnest
Sign Indicates Dangerous Elephants
She Invested Daily Earnings

Now see how many four-word phrases you can come up with in five minutes using the letters:

P A F T

When you have finished, turn to page 22 to rate your performance.

Hit the headlines

Imagine you are working for a newspaper and have been given the following story:

While sunbathing on the deck of a small boat three weeks ago, a 40-year-old woman from San Diego, California, lost her wedding ring. Today, her husband went fishing near the same spot. Cleaning his catch, he was astounded to find the missing wedding band inside one of the fish.

Your editor asks you to supply as many witty headlines as you can. You have a ten-minute deadline. When you have written your suggestions, turn to page 22 for some potential solutions.

BETWEEN THE LINES

On a large sheet of paper, sketch out several pairs of simple parallel lines. Now draw a series of pictures, incorporating a set of these lines in each one, as shown at right.

For example, a pair of lines could become the bars of an electric heater, the skis of a daring downhill racer, the chimney stacks of a large industrial building, the masts on a small sail boat, or the legs of a wading flamingo.

See how many suitable images you can produce in just five minutes, then turn to the solutions box on page 23 to assess your skills.

1a

Speakeasy
*Think up as many amusing,
perceptive, or interesting
captions for these three pictures
as you can. Allow yourself ten
minutes for this test. See the
solutions box below.*

Picture preferences
*Out of each pair of
pictures, which one
do you prefer? Check
your answers in the
solutions box below.*

4a

SOLUTIONS

Creative connections
The answers that follow are the most obvious ones.
Give yourself one point for every answer that
matches the suggestions given here:
1. house **2.** sea **3.** foot **4.** cob **5.** tax **6.** stone
7. man **8.** jack **9.** over **10.** sun
The number of correct answers you gave indicates
your ability to think fluently.

You may have found an original solution, not
listed here, that also works. Originality means you
have been thinking divergently as well as fluently.
Give yourself two extra points for every original
solution you came up with. Add up your score.

A score of more than 7 suggests your ability to
use and interpret words creatively is good and your
verbal dexterity is already well developed. If,
however, you scored less than 7 you need not
worry—you will be able to develop and improve this
skill by making up similar word games and
practicing them. A score of 10 or over suggests you
are already highly creative in this area.

Letter lengtheners
You may have come up with phrases such as:
Plant A Fir Tree
People Are Funny Things
Purchase Apples For Tommy
Pitch All Five Tents
Give yourself one point for each phrase you devised,
whether it is on the list or not. If you scored 10 or more,
you are thinking very fluently. This kind of test is not
easy, so if you scored less than 10 this simply means you
need to exercise your verbal fluency more often.

Hit the headlines
Here are some examples of suitable titles:
Net Results
Caught in the Tract
A Fishy Tale
The Golden Find
If you came up with 5 or more headlines, you are
thinking fluently. In the Guilford test from which this is
adapted, you would also be given points for the

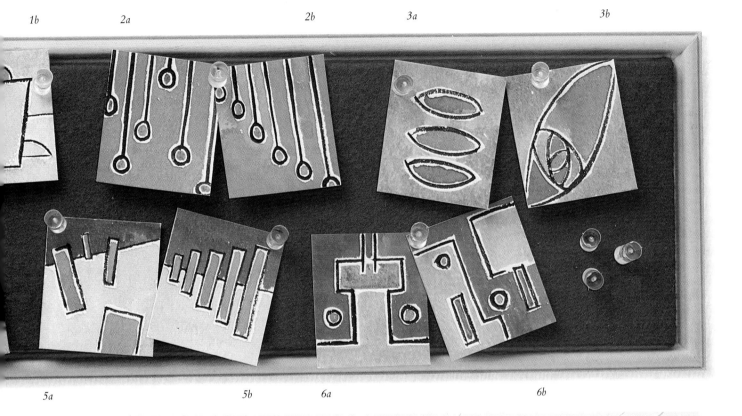

1b　　　*2a*　　　　　*2b*　　　*3a*　　　　　*3b*

5a　　　　　　*5b*　　*6a*　　　　　*6b*

cleverness of your titles. Adding an extra point for every title that includes a play on words, 7 is a good score.

Between the lines

You don't have to be a great artist to be able to think visually. You need only to look at objects in as many different ways as possible, so that you see all the creative options in something as simple as a pair of parallel lines. If you drew more than 10 pictures, you have a good ability to use images creatively. If you drew fewer than 10, try to improve your score by practicing the exercise in your spare moments.

You can also improve your visual skills by using other simple shapes as starting points. For example, take a button and outline it 20 times. Invent 20 different ways to fill in the circles with pictures or patterns.

Speakeasy

This test is measured in two ways. The total number of captions you compose indicates the fluency of your ideas—the more the merrier. The cleverness of the captions you create illustrates your originality. Score one point for every caption, and another point for each one that is particularly catchy or clever. If you score fewer than 12, you may want to work on this side of creative thinking. Between 12 and 18 indicates a high degree of fluency. If your score is higher than 18, your creative fluency is already well developed.

Picture preferences

Which pictures did you prefer? The most creative choices, based on the answers to a test called the Barron-Welsh Figure Preference Test, are: 1a, 2a, 3b, 4b, 5a, 6b.

These are the less ordered pictures in each pair. If you chose mainly these, you prefer complexity and asymmetry to simplicity and balance, indicating a tendency to think in a creative way. People whose thought processes are creative tend to prefer disorder, possibly because it frees them to impose their own original order on the material.

WHOLE-BRAIN THINKING

ALMOST EVERYONE WHO has read a book or article on popular psychology knows that the brain has two halves—the right hemisphere and the left hemisphere, often called the right and left brain. Modern thinking on this matter began with the so-called split-brain studies carried out in the early 1960s by Nobel Prize winner Roger Sperry at the California Institute of Technology. In studying epileptics whose brain hemispheres had been surgically separated to reduce seizures, Sperry found that the two halves of the brain contribute differently to the process of thinking.

Over the next decade, psychologists determined that the left brain is used most for analytical thought and for verbal functions such as speaking, writing, and reading. It deals with information bit by bit, breaking it down into one-step-at-a-time logical sequences. Conversely, the right brain is nonverbal or mute. It deals with images and is particularly good at recognizing complex visual patterns that may not be logically linked. The right brain grasps these pictures as a whole. For example, if you try to recognize the figure of Waldo in the popular *Where's Waldo?* books by looking at the whole picture, you are making use of the right brain. In contrast, the left-brain approach would be to examine and compare each person in the scene.

The idea that differences between people could be related to how they use one or the other brain hemisphere carried wide popular appeal. Some studies went so far as to claim that, in most people, the left brain hemisphere was dominant, while the right brain played a minor role. This left-brained bias, theorists argued, was the inevitable outcome of Western education with its heavy emphasis on reading, writing, arithmetic, and rational, analytic thought. Lawyers, writers, tax experts, doctors, and bookkeepers, it was said, were left-brained, whereas poets, musicians, and dancers—the creative minority—relied on the right hemisphere.

Dual contribution

Today, most psychologists see this as a dangerous oversimplification. The current thinking is that both the right and left brains contribute specialized capabilities, and that only by using the whole brain can a person think creatively. For instance, as you read these pages, your right brain hemisphere is responsible for such activities as understanding metaphor and maintaining narrative structure. At the same time, your left hemisphere is interpreting syntax and deriving meaning from words.

Although research has shown that the right brain does have a limited verbal capability, and can handle simple messages, the ability to use language is still the most profound difference between the left and the right hemispheres. But the contribution of the right brain is very important indeed. It handles complex information that can't be fully captured in words. Consider a simple scene of two young girls

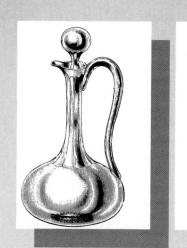

ART MADE EASY

According to California art teacher Betty Edwards, the right brain has the ability to draw, but the analytical left brain tends to interfere. To demonstrate this, she has her students copy a drawing with the picture held upside down. Because the image is not recognizable to the left brain, the right brain is unimpeded as it produces a pleasing and surprisingly accurate copy.

Try this for yourself. Copy the vase on the left first, then draw the upside-down version. The second method should produce a truer copy.

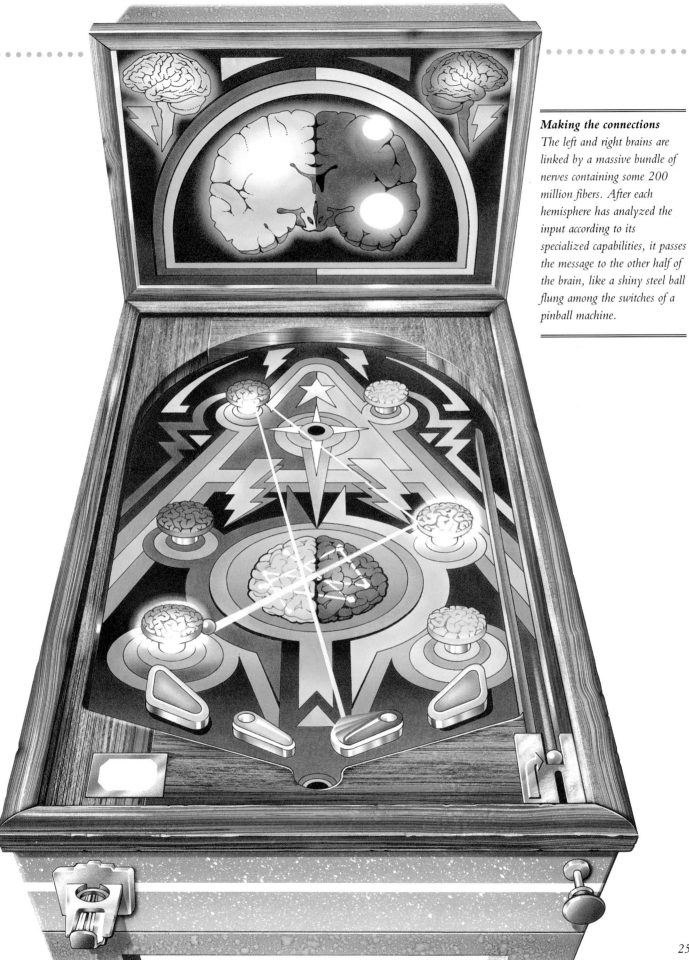

Making the connections
The left and right brains are linked by a massive bundle of nerves containing some 200 million fibers. After each hemisphere has analyzed the input according to its specialized capabilities, it passes the message to the other half of the brain, like a shiny steel ball flung among the switches of a pinball machine.

playing catch in a park. Each time a child throws the ball, the other one estimates its speed, angle of flight, and the wind speed, and moves to intercept the ball. Even if she later earned a college degree in physics, she might never produce equations that would predict the ball's flight, but the right brain can judge such things almost automatically.

Although the left and right brains must work together to perform a task efficiently, it is still true that one or the other hemisphere is more active in most people. Some types of everyday behavior can tell you which of the hemispheres you naturally favor. For instance, in assembling a product purchased in kit form, you reveal a left-brain bias if you rely on the written step-by-step instructions. In contrast, a person with strong right-brain input may prefer to follow diagrams or pictures.

Learn to "think right"
Many simple, nonverbal activities can stimulate right-brain thinking in people whose left hemisphere is dominant. Listening to music or taking a long bath are two examples. These activities seem to lull the left brain into indolence. Another approach is to occupy the left hemisphere with a menial chore that gets it out of the right brain's way. In his book *The Inner Game of Tennis*, tennis professional Tim Gallwey suggests just such a trick.

Gallwey tells his students to say the word "bounce" as the ball hits the court in front of them, and "hit" as they strike it with the racket. This is enough to divert the left brain, and keep it from dictating a list of logical commands. The right brain can then help the player hit the ball instinctively.

Most people are not aware of which hemisphere is dominant at a particular time. But recent advances in computer science have resulted in a scan that reveals the brain's activity as color images on a computer screen. This Computerized Automated Psychophysiological (CAP) scan has confirmed that dominance constantly shifts between the hemispheres. Now some scientists predict that with CAP-scan practice, people will be able to learn how to shift their thinking from one side of the brain to the other at will. If CAP-scan use becomes widespread, you might be able to train yourself to "think right" or "think left".

HOW INTUITIVE ARE YOU?

Intuition is a catch-all word that is used to describe thinking processes that cannot be explained logically—the sudden flash of right-brain insight that leads to a new idea, your hunch about whether a job interview will result in an offer of employment, or the gut feeling that tells you which horse is going to win the Kentucky Derby.

Myths about intuition abound, but in the case of the popular notion about women being more intuitive than men there does seem to be some basis in fact. Research has shown that female brains have more connections between the right and left hemispheres, allowing women to take in and cross-connect different kinds of information more easily. Women are therefore better equipped to perceive the subtle nuances of other people's behavior, and then unconsciously evaluate these perceptions.

To see how developed your own intuition is, try the following test. Answer each question with **A** often, **B** sometimes, **C** rarely, or **D** never.

1. Do your first impressions of people turn out to be an accurate assessment of their character?

2. Do the events depicted in your dreams ever occur later in real life?

3. Do friends and colleagues seem to value you as a good listener?

4. Did you have a make-believe playmate when you were a child?

5. Have you thought about someone you have not heard from in a long time, only to be contacted by that person shortly afterward?

6. When you make an important decision, do you base it largely on your gut feelings about what would be the right thing do?

7. Do you take on a series of problems and later discover that while your reasoning may sometimes have been faulty, you managed to reach the right conclusion with surprising frequency?

8. Do you like to spend time alone?

9. Can you sense when someone close to you is worried or unhappy?

10. If you are spending an evening alone at home, do you resist the temptation to switch on the television?

How do you score?

Now you have completed the test, score your results. For every **A**, give yourself 4 points; for every **B**, 3 points; for every **C**, 2 points; and for every **D**, 1 point.

If you scored:

30 - 40 You have highly developed intuitive skills, which play a large part in the way you run your life.

20 - 29 This indicates you have considerable intuitive potential. In order to make the most of this potential, however, you need to give that side of your thinking a freer rein.

10 - 19 You are not using your intuition as much as you could. Set aside at least 15 minutes a day to practice relaxation exercises, and learn to pay attention to any flashes of insight or hunches you may have.

Read through these additional comments on the test questions to help you determine where your intuitive strengths lie and how your skills might best be improved in this area.

1. Making an accurate initial judgment of people is a good sign of intuitive potential.

2. The symbolic language of dreams can be confusing, but dreams can sometimes reaffirm thoughts you had at an intuitive level.

3. Being able to listen sensitively to other people is linked closely with being aware of intuitive feelings within yourself.

4. Children who show imagination by inventing playmates to keep them company may well carry their strong intuitive skills into adult life.

5. When someone writes or calls unexpectedly, you may have intuitively anticipated his or her intention to make contact.

6. If you have confidence in your inner voice, you are naturally intuitive.

7. Both intuition and reasoning are useful in solving problems. Intuition may supply an insight that leads to a solution, but you should always test such ideas before you act on them.

8. Individuals who relish the quiet of their own thoughts are often open to intuitive suggestions.

9. Having a feel for the emotional states of others is a strong sign of intuition.

10. Those who spend much of their leisure time relying on outside stimulation are not giving their intuition ample opportunity to develop.

THE CREATIVE PERSONALITY

ACCORDING TO IRISH PLAYWRIGHT George Bernard Shaw, "The artist will let his wife starve, his children go barefoot, and his mother drudge for his living at 70, sooner than work at anything but his art." Few people would want to emulate that degree of cruelty and obsession in the name of creativity. But there are certain personality traits common to most imaginative individuals, and prominent among them are, as Shaw suggests, a single-minded devotion to a chosen field and a firm belief in the ultimate value of their work.

Although creative people are often portrayed as dreamy and wayward, they are, in fact, more likely to be persistent and dedicated. Psychologist Anne Roe studied 64 eminent scientists at work and reported that they all had a "driving absorption in their work," often putting in long hours because they would rather work than do anything else. Motivated by a zeal that at times amounted to fanaticism, the scientists were unusually productive. The quality and quantity, Roe discovered, tended to be related. People who do the most work often also produce the best.

Independent self-starters
Studies show that innovators usually need to work independently. Although they are interested in the ideas of others and may be influenced by people they admire, such individuals are also single-minded and self-sufficient. Generally preferring to work on their own, creative people do not wait for the instructions or the plans of others.

A degree of nonconformity—sometimes spilling over into eccentricity—characterizes many original thinkers. Einstein, for example, occasionally appeared in public minus one sock. At a deeper level, some creators seem to be out of step with their times because their ideas are too advanced; only after their deaths are they considered brilliant. Nonconformers, however, usually persist with their ideas, no matter how unfashionable they may seem to their contemporaries.

Flexible interpretation
Another character trait commonly associated with creativity is what psychologist John S. Dacey calls "tolerance for ambiguity." Less

Changing perspective
Can you spot the large face hidden among the many smaller examples that make up this image? The ability to look at pictures, words, or ideas from different angles is a trait often found in creative people.

creative people dislike situations in which they are unsure how they are meant to react. An innovative person will enjoy the challenge. Confronted by a work of avant-garde art, for example, people low on creativity may feel disturbed that the object gives them no clue as to how to respond: Are they supposed to laugh or be shocked or find it beautiful? The creative person will enjoy trying out various possible responses, and will feel no need to resolve any contradictions.

This enjoyment of ambiguity goes hand in hand with a willingness to take risks. The creative person is not afraid to confront new situations or paralyzed by the possibility of failure.

The long-term view

Research into the creative personality has revealed a wide range of other shared characteristics. For example, creative individuals tend to have a preference for long-term rewards rather than short-term gains. At Stanford University, researcher Walter Mischel found that this characteristic develops in childhood. Children who are better at waiting for larger rewards, rather than settling for a small one offered on the spot, are more likely to grow up to be creatively productive.

While reward is important for creative people, it does not always consist of material incentives such as money. A study of poets found that their work actually deteriorated when they were paid for it directly; the payment appeared to diminish the pure joy of creativity. Perhaps the poets would have been better motivated by less tangible rewards such as praise, respect, or admiration.

Beauty and the best

A well-developed aesthetic sense is another trait of creative people. It may seem obvious that artistic expression calls for an appreciation of beauty, but this same sensibility can play a part in scientific work. Mathematicians prize the elegance, as well as the accuracy, of a correct solution, and may find aesthetic pleasure in the symmetry of an equation.

Many researchers have investigated the relationship between intelligence (as measured by IQ tests) and creativity. Most psychologists agree that the two things are not the same. Psychologists Jacob Getzels and Philip W. Jackson devised a test for

adolescents that aimed to illustrate the difference. The teenagers were divided into groups distinguishing those who showed signs of being highly creative from those who simply had high IQs. They were all asked to look at a picture of a businessman in an airplane seat, then both groups were asked to write a few sentences about what might be happening in the picture.

Most of the high-IQ group wrote that the man was returning from a successful business trip. He felt happy, they said, and looked forward to seeing his family. However, the creative teenagers were more likely to make up a less conventional scenario. One wrote that the man had just won a divorce from his wife, whom he could not bear because she put on so much cold cream at night. According to this youngster's elaborate story, the wife's head had a tendency to skid across the pillow and collide with that of her husband, who was already at work on a formula for a skid-proof face cream.

The differences between these stories suggest that creative individuals tend to

Blend of talents

Creative people often refuse to be constrained by traditional male-female roles; instead they exploit the strong points of both sexes.

THE MALE-FEMALE MIX

Some psychologists see creativity as having a link to androgyny—the possession of both male and female personality traits. In a creative person, they argue, qualities that are usually associated with the female sex, such as sensitivity and intuition, are blended with those traditionally viewed as manly, such as determination and logic.

Express the feminine

In a study of highly creative male architects, psychologist Donald W. MacKinnon concluded, "The more creative a person is the more he reveals an openness to his own feelings and emotions, a sensitive intellect and understanding self-awareness, and wide-ranging interests, including many which in the American culture are thought of as feminine. In the realm of sexual identification and interest, our creative subjects appear to give more expression to the feminine side of their nature than do less creative persons."

This does not imply that a creative man is effeminate, or a creative woman masculine. It means instead that, in any situation, creative people have a wider choice of personality traits to draw from, rather than being restricted to typical male or female roles. They are thus freer to express themselves in whatever way they think is appropriate.

be more off-beat and lively in their ideas, whereas intelligent, but uncreative, thinkers tend to be rather more conventional.

Not too surprisingly then, it seems that a high IQ does not necessarily guarantee a creative personality, although creative people often score above average in IQ tests. A scientific genius such as Einstein, who managed to combine a towering intelligence with prolific creativity, was thus a rare exception to the rule.

New knowledge versus old

However, neither Einstein nor English naturalist Charles Darwin—another frontier-breaking scientist—did well in school, a failing common to quite a number of creative people. As American writer Thomas G. West comments in his book *In the*

Mind's Eye, "Exceptional people are sometimes far better at creating new knowledge than in absorbing and retaining old knowledge . . . some of the most extraordinary minds may be found at the bottom of the class." Resist the temptation to assess yourself in terms of scholarly achievements. In some ways, the less shackled your mind is by traditional learning, the greater your chances of coming up with novel ideas.

No one has all the ideal characteristics of a creative personality in equal measure. The test that follows on pages 32 and 33 will help you identify which of the traits associated with creativity you are best endowed with and where your weaknesses lie. Gaining a clearer picture of your particular characteristics should give you a solid foundation on which to build your creative skills.

DO YOU HAVE A CREATIVE PERSONALITY?

This questionnaire assesses you for five personality traits associated with creativity: risktaking, independence, nonconformity, productivity, and persistence. Answer the questions as honestly as you can, giving a "yes" or "no" answer response to every question, even if the answer seems only roughly appropriate. Then refer to the "How do you score?" box opposite for an interpretation.

1. Do you always keep to the speed limit when you're driving on the freeway? ....❏

2. Are you at your best working as part of a team under a boss?..............❏

3. Are you ever the most casually dressed person at a formal occasion?.......❏

4. Do you get confused when you have to work on several things at once? ...❏

5. Do you often find yourself thinking about work problems even when you're at home? ....❏

6. If you had a brilliant new business idea that you were sure would make big money, would you take out a second loan to launch it? ....❏

7. Would you enjoy taking vacations on your own? ...❏

8. Do you think that bad laws should be broken? ....❏

9. Once you've finished a job, do you go straight on to the next one, whether or not it's urgent? ....❏

10. Are you someone who feels if a job is worth doing, it's worth doing well?.......❏

11. Would it bother you if you owed more on your credit cards than you could pay off immediately?........❏

12. You have decided to redecorate your home and can afford an interior designer. Would you still prefer to plan the decor yourself? ....❏

13. Do you like the idea of working in a job where there are set ways of doing things?............................❏

14. Are you ever at a loss to find ways of filling your spare time? ....❏

15. If you broke a household appliance, such as a toaster, would you try to fix it before calling in an expert?.........❏

16. Would you still read a book by an author you have always liked even if it got bad reviews? ....❏

17. Does the thought of traveling alone in a foreign country scare you?...........❏

18. Do you think of several solutions to a problem before settling on one?.....❏

19. If you invented a new household gadget, would you try to produce and sell it yourself?........................❏

20. Do you find you get easily distracted from the task at hand?...................❏

21. Seeing a short cut across a park lawn, would you take it even though there is a "keep off the grass" sign nearby?...........❏

22. If you were offered a berth on a round-the-world yachting trip, and you had no commitments to stop you, would you take it? ...❏

23. Are you more likely to buy clothes because they are comfortable than because they are fashionable?........❏

24. Do you think it will be difficult to fill your time when you retire?..............❏

25. If a dish you order in a restaurant doesn't taste right, do you send it back? ....❏

26. Would you invest a substantial amount of your savings in a stock if you were promised it would make you a fortune? ....❏

27. Do you prefer to take vacations where everything is organized for you? ....❑

28. Do you hold an opinion regardless of what other people think? ....❑

29. Are you someone who tends to steam ahead with activities, leaving everyone else trailing behind? ....❑

30. Would you say that you get bored with carrying out repetitive tasks? ....❑

31. When you have important guests for dinner, do you always serve dishes you've cooked before? .....❑

32. Do you think that people should work out their problems for themselves rather than seek help from others? ....❑

33. Would it bother you to see people drinking fine wine out of old coffee mugs? ....❑

34. Do you find that there aren't enough hours in the day for all the things that you want to do? ....❑

35. If you broke a treasured object, would you throw it out rather than mend it?. ..❑

36. Does it worry you if someone dislikes you? ......❑

37. Do you think it's better to keep your opinions to yourself if they might offend someone? ....❑

38. Do you generally complete your projects on schedule? ,......................❑

39. Do you dislike the thought of taking on a task that involves sorting out lots of tricky details? ......❑

40. Would you allow your hairdresser to give you a radical new hair style? .....❑

41. In a discussion, do you keep on arguing your case until you're sure everyone sees your point of view? ....❑

42. Do you tend to feel uncomfortable in a room full of strangers? ....❑

43. Do other people often think you are weird? ....❑

44. If you won 10 million dollars, do you think you'd keep on working? ....❑

45. Would you go bungee jumping from the top of a bridge if someone offered you the opportunity? ......❑

46. Would you rather remain in an unsatisfactory relationship than be on your own? ....❑

47. Do you think only married couples should have children? ....❑

48. Do you enjoy solving problems just for the sake of exercising your mind? ......❑

49. When you're working on a fascinating project, do you find it difficult to tear yourself away? ....❑

50. Do you eat and drink whatever you enjoy, regardless of how this might affect your health? ....❑

HOW DO YOU SCORE?

The five traits assessed by the questions at left are common in highly creative people.
In each category, a high score is 7 or more points, a low score is below 4 points. Identifying weak areas may prompt you to work on these aspects of your personality.

Risktaking: Score one point for each "yes" to questions 6, 22, 26, 40, 45, and 50, and one for each "no" to questions 1, 11, 17, and 31. High scorers welcome change and accept the possibility of failure. Low scorers need to grow less dependent on the familiar, and to be more open to fresh, challenging experiences.

Independence: Score one for each "yes" to 7, 12, 19, and 32, and one for each "no" to 2, 13, 27, 36, 42, and 46. High scorers work best on their own initiative. If your score was low, you need to develop more self-sufficiency and learn not to wait for instructions before you act.

Nonconformity: Score one for each "yes" to 3, 8, 16, 21, 23, 28, and 43, and one for each "no" to 33, 37, and 47. High scorers are rebellious and not influenced by fashion. If you're a low scorer, free your creativity by learning to apply independent thought—not blind obedience—to rules and social pressures.

Productivity: Score one for each "yes" to 9, 18, 29, 34, 38, 44, and 48, and one for each "no" to 4, 14, and 24. High scorers are prolific, tending to produce as much work as possible. Low scorers are overcritical and their lack of confidence inhibits their energy. Give yourself a chance to create before you criticize; demanding perfection can block creative flow.

Persistence: Score one point for each "yes" to 5, 10, 15, 25, and 49, and one for each "no" to 20, 30, 35, 39, and 41. High scorers never give up, they have a driving absorption in their work and may be fanatical about their pursuits. If you scored low, be more insistent on achieving your goals and don't be discouraged by any setbacks.

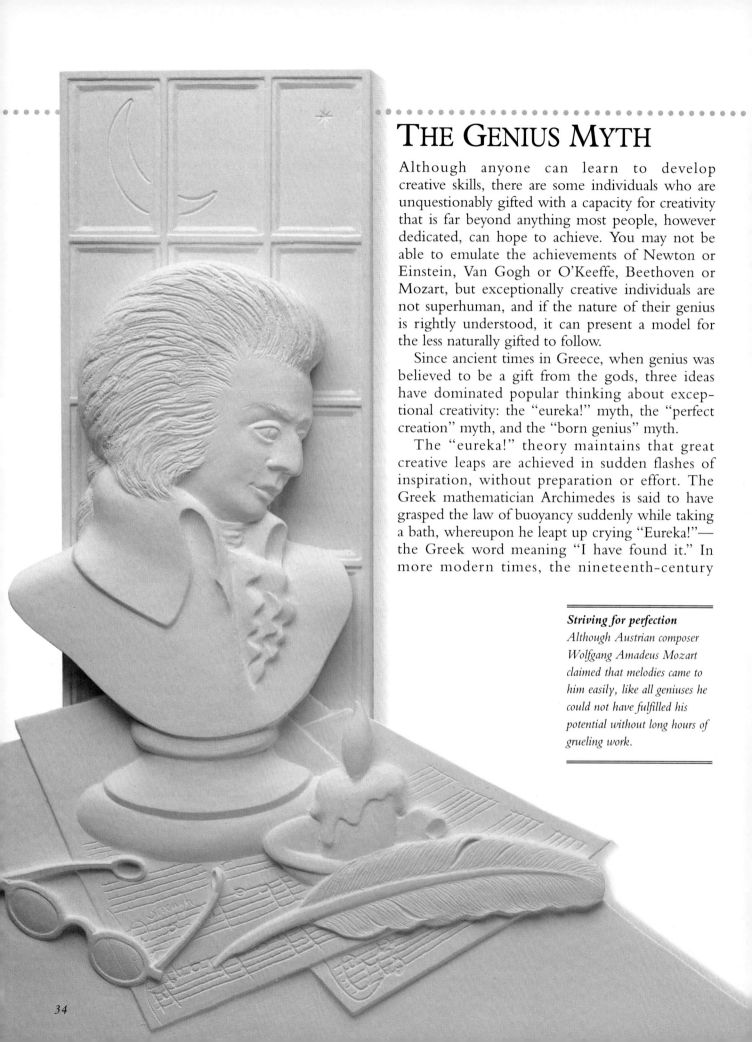

THE GENIUS MYTH

Although anyone can learn to develop creative skills, there are some individuals who are unquestionably gifted with a capacity for creativity that is far beyond anything most people, however dedicated, can hope to achieve. You may not be able to emulate the achievements of Newton or Einstein, Van Gogh or O'Keeffe, Beethoven or Mozart, but exceptionally creative individuals are not superhuman, and if the nature of their genius is rightly understood, it can present a model for the less naturally gifted to follow.

Since ancient times in Greece, when genius was believed to be a gift from the gods, three ideas have dominated popular thinking about exceptional creativity: the "eureka!" myth, the "perfect creation" myth, and the "born genius" myth.

The "eureka!" theory maintains that great creative leaps are achieved in sudden flashes of inspiration, without preparation or effort. The Greek mathematician Archimedes is said to have grasped the law of buoyancy suddenly while taking a bath, whereupon he leapt up crying "Eureka!"—the Greek word meaning "I have found it." In more modern times, the nineteenth-century

Striving for perfection
Although Austrian composer Wolfgang Amadeus Mozart claimed that melodies came to him easily, like all geniuses he could not have fulfilled his potential without long hours of grueling work.

English naturalist Charles Darwin recorded that he conceptualized his famous theory of evolution through natural selection within a few minutes of having read an essay by English economist Thomas Malthus. History abounds with similar tales.

Yet, these stories of people envisioning a brilliant idea in a sudden flash of insight often overlook the long months, or even years, of thought and creativity that led up to the moment of discovery. American psychologist Howard Gruber maintains that even the most eminently creative mind needs to be immersed in a subject for at least 10 years before inspiration strikes. Darwin, for example, developed half a dozen theories similar to evolutionary selection in the years before he formulated his ground-breaking theory.

Whole and complete
Similar to the "eureka!" myth is the notion of "perfect creation," which holds that great works spring whole and complete from the minds of geniuses with no need for revision or amendment. Many creators, enjoying the air of mastery this idea projects, have promulgated it themselves. The English Romantic poet Samuel Taylor Coleridge, for example, claimed to have composed his poem *Kubla Khan* in a dreamlike drug-induced state, "without any sensation or consciousness of effort." Research has shown, however, that he wrote at least one draft before his dream experience.

Geniuses in fact differ in their working methods. While Ludwig van Beethoven and American poet T. S. Eliot constantly revised their work, others, including Russian composer Igor Stravinsky, did not. Either way, they could have achieved nothing without concentrated effort.

Learning for life
Finally, there is the contention that "geniuses are born not made." Advocates of this theory claim that exceptionally creative people are born ready to accomplish great things and have little to learn from life. Yet the creative talents of perhaps the most famous of all young geniuses, Wolfgang Amadeus Mozart, who began writing music at the age of five, improved markedly over the years, suggesting that even his extraordinary innate abilities improved with hard work and time. Nor are all

GENIUS AND MADNESS

Many well-known creative geniuses have suffered some form of psychosis. The list includes artists Vincent van Gogh and Wassily Kandinsky, scientists Isaac Newton and Michael Faraday, writers Edgar Allan Poe, Ezra Pound, and Sylvia Plath, and philosophers Arthur Schopenhauer and Friedrich Nietzsche.

Because the products of genius are often unusual and ahead of their time, many other exceptionally creative people have been wrongly dismissed as mad by their contemporaries, only to be revered in a later age. Many of the people who knew the nineteenth-century poet Emily Dickinson, for example, considered her odd because of her powerful desire for solitude; yet today she is regarded as one of America's greatest writers.

Modern psychology suggests that creativity, far from being an outgrowth of insanity, is an outlet that allows some emotionally troubled people to stay sane. When creative people become truly unbalanced, their productivity diminishes, because mental illness generates high anxiety levels that disrupt creative output.

geniuses child prodigies. Vincent van Gogh only began to paint at the age of 30, after failing first as an apprentice art dealer and then as a preacher.

The lesson to be drawn from this survey of genius is that creativity always involves application and hard work, even for the most gifted. Contrary to popular belief, geniuses are not necessarily eccentric, childish, selfish, or introverted. They do, however, express a high level of commitment to their work. To perfect his drawing technique, for example, the Renaissance artist Leonardo da Vinci drew more than a thousand hands, and Darwin devoted eight years of his life at the height of his fame to the study of the humble barnacle.

Many ordinary people have known some form of eureka experience—a moment when the solution to a problem appeared out of the blue, even if it was only a clever way to improvise a bookshelf or to solve a puzzle. But genius combines this inspiration with an accumulation of knowledge, single-minded dedication, exceptional motivation, and, of course, unusual talents. The results are original creations of significance to the world.

ALTERED STATES

S INCE EARLIEST TIMES, people have gone to great
lengths to achieve states of ecstasy and eupho-
ria, which would free them, however temporarily,
from the drudgery of ordinary waking consciousness. Those seeking such altered states of mind
have relied on a wide variety of methods—
everything from ingesting hallucinogens to
fasting and practicing meditation.

Yet everyone experiences at least
one rather dramatic altered state
every day when they go to sleep.
And although they may not be
fully aware of it, many people
routinely alter their mental
condition through the
intake of alcohol, caffeine,
or nicotine.

New insights
From time to time over
the years, people have
stepped forward to claim
a connection between
altered states of con-
sciousness, particularly
those that are drug-
induced, and creativity.
They have argued that
changes in consciousness
bring about a special vision
of the world—a "cleansing
[of] the gates of perception,"
according to the English poet
and mystic William Blake—and
are able to release the creative
imagination from the shackles of
common sense and logic.

But psychologists who have carried
out objective studies of altered states of
consciousness find no evidence that they
enhance creativity in any remarkable way. The

Changing consciousness

*Traditionally a feature of
religions based on Eastern
philosophies, meditation seeks*

*to provide tranquillity by
teaching techniques that empty
the mind of worldly distractions.*

presence of an altered state during a creative act appears to be largely incidental. If an altered state does affect a person's creative output, it will mostly do so indirectly. A musician, for example, may take drugs believing that they will make him or her a more creative performer. Any increased creativity, however, will be due more to the musician's belief in the drugs and the heightened confidence this provides than to the drugs themselves.

But even if no magic pill, potion, or meditative technique will automatically produce or increase creativity, that is not to say that such methods have no effect at all. Studies have shown, for example, that some drug stimulants—even commonplace ones, such as caffeine—can make people more productive, and productivity is a vital part of creativity.

Artificial inspiration

Depressant drugs such as alcohol, on the other hand, have a complex effect on creativity. Alcohol can help the creative process by lessening inhibitions and releasing ideas that might normally be blocked. Yet when consumed in more than modest quantities, alcohol interferes with the mental processes that are needed for solving complex problems, evaluating ideas, and performing accurately, and thus may reduce the quality of creative output.

The effects of hallucinogenic drugs on creativity are also ambiguous. Some people feel these drugs boost their ability to come up with original ideas and produce creative work, and, indeed, certain works of art have been produced under the influence of such substances. Yet, although hallucinogens fill the mind with unusual imagery and perceptions, they do not provide the discipline needed for creativity: A poem or picture created under the influence of a hallucinogenic drug (or of excess alcohol) tends to appear incomprehensible rather than creative and beautiful. So despite the claims of some users, the scientific evidence that drugs enhance creativity is, at best, insufficient.

IN A "BROWN STUDY"

The English writer Aldous Huxley developed a unique meditative technique that enabled him to enter repeatedly into an altered state of deep reflection. Once in this state of mind, he was able to summon his memories, order his thoughts, and, in his own words, "explore the range and extent of existence."

To change his state of consciousness, Huxley always sat in a particular chair. He would begin by bowing his head, closing his eyes, and physically relaxing his body. As he did so, he withdrew his thoughts from any external stimuli.

It took Huxley about five minutes to induce a state of reverie, which he called his "brown study." Surprisingly, he was able to carry out other functions, such as answering the phone, while in this reverie, although he would have no memory of these activities afterward.

Huxley described one "brown study" session in which he decided to focus his mind on color. He reported that he gradually became so "lost" in a sea of color that he felt he no longer had an identity of his own. Huxley believed such intense experiences helped him as a novelist because they enabled him to explore imaginative possibilities otherwise closed to him.

HAVE A BRAIN WAVE

Using a procedure called an electroencephalogram (EEG), scientists can determine the state of a person's brain activity. Electrodes placed on the scalp record the electrical output of the brain as wave patterns.

Although irregular much of the time, these patterns are sometimes quite distinct. By studying them, scientists have established that particular brain waves correspond to particular mental states.

In other words, each of your mental states—deep sleep, for example, or meditation—exhibits its own characteristic type of electrical activity in your brain that can be objectively measured.

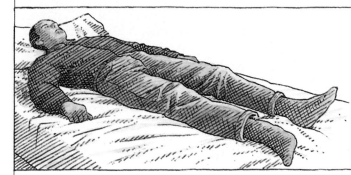

Alpha waves
This type of brain wave occurs at frequencies of 8 to 13 cycles per second. Alpha waves are found during states of hypnosis and when people are deeply relaxed but awake, as in meditation.

Beta waves
Brain waves that have frequencies of 14 to 50 cycles per second are called beta waves. These waves occur during wakefulness and accompany most mental activities.

Theta waves
Children's brains are rich in theta waves, emitted at 4 to 7 cycles per second. Theta waves rarely occur in adults, except in the hypnagogic state that occurs between sleep and consciousness.

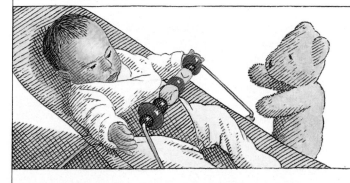

Delta waves
The slow brain rhythms of deep sleep are called delta waves. They include all waves below 3.5 cycles per second and can be as low as 1 cycle per second.

There is evidence, however, that meditation techniques may encourage creativity, at least in limited ways. Like alcohol, meditation can diminish your mental inhibitions, thus helping you escape from thought processes that have been tying your thinking in knots and keeping you from perceiving solutions to problems. Yet unlike alcohol, meditation does not present a risk to your health.

Meditation also appears to be beneficial in helping people recover from the mental fatigue caused by stressful work, and it contributes positively to what Graham Wallas called the "incubation" period of thinking (see page 14).

The scientific study of altered states associated with meditation and sleep has been transformed by the electroencephalogram (EEG), which measures electrical activity in the brain. Through the use of EEGs, scientists have linked a type of brain wave pattern—called alpha waves—to deep relaxation (see box opposite). This discovery has led in turn to the development of biofeedback, a technique that aids meditation.

Employing electronic equipment similar to that of an EEG machine, biofeedback enables the user of the equipment to measure his or her own brain waves. Many people have found that once they are able to gauge their brain waves, they can learn to induce the state of body and mind required to achieve alpha waves—or deep relaxation.

You can induce an alpha wave state without a biofeedback machine by using relaxation techniques. To do this, lie down in a comfortable position and close your eyes. Then, starting with your feet and working up toward your head, imagine each part of your body in turn becoming relaxed and heavy. By the time you have reached your head, you should feel completely relaxed and may well be producing alpha waves.

KEKULE'S SNAKE

Nineteenth-century German chemist Friedrich August Kekule von Stradonitz spent many years exploring the structures of organic molecules, then one of the most puzzling areas of science. Of particular interest was an aromatic liquid called benzene, whose molecular structure had long eluded detection. One night in 1865, Kekule was sitting dozing by the fire when he "dreamed" he saw the atoms of the benzene molecule whirling around until they resolved themselves into the image of a snake biting its own tail. Kekule awoke convinced that he had cracked the problem of the structure of the benzene molecule. His vision had told him that benzene atoms must form a closed ring, an inspired breakthrough in organic chemistry.

An altered state rich in theta waves occurs just before you fall asleep and before you fully waken. This "hypnagogic state," as it is called, is characterized by a kind of drowsiness in which images of almost hallucinatory clarity may appear. It is like dreaming while being awake. Most individuals who report experiencing "in a dream" a sudden answer to a problem that they have been thinking about for a long time, more than likely received the inspiration not while dreaming, but while in the dreamlike hypnagogic state.

Hypnagogic states occur either naturally or not at all. The way of encouraging them is to ensure that you waken naturally, then allow yourself to drowse a while without distractions such as the sound of a radio. Above all, avoid setting an alarm clock, since the sudden awakening will destroy any possibility of a hypnagogic experience.

Dream sleep is the most ubiquitous form of altered state. In dreams, the imagination is liberated from rational constraints and given a free rein to generate stories and images. However, because it cannot be harnessed in any useful way, this nightly burst of creativity doesn't often lead anywhere. Most dreams are forgotten instantly on waking, and those that are remembered go unused because the conscious, logical side of the mind finds it very difficult to make sense of them.

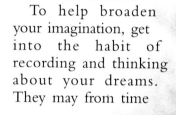

To help broaden your imagination, get into the habit of recording and thinking about your dreams. They may from time

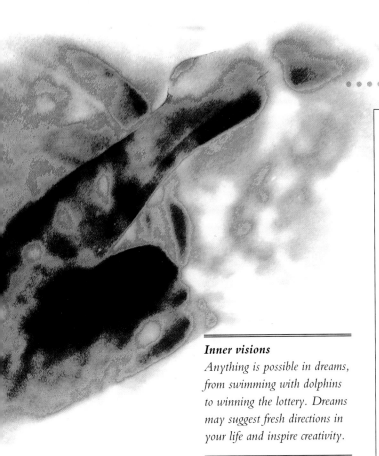

Inner visions
Anything is possible in dreams, from swimming with dolphins to winning the lottery. Dreams may suggest fresh directions in your life and inspire creativity.

DREAM ON

Although the average sleeper has about five dream sessions every night, many people are unable to remember a single dream. Even dreams recalled vividly on waking usually vanish from your consciousness during the day. By making an effort to remember and mull over your dreams, however, you may discover new and unusual insights into your life. Here are some steps to aid this process:

1. Keep a notebook and pen by your bedside.

2. Before going to sleep, say firmly, "I will remember at least one dream."

3. Set your alarm for 15 minutes earlier than usual. Your last dream generally happens just before you would normally awake. By waking slightly earlier you may catch yourself in the middle of a dream.

4. As soon as you wake up, write down any dream fragments that you can remember. Or use a tape recorder, making sure in advance that you are familiar with its controls so that you can use it even when you are half asleep.

5. Later in the day, read what you have written or listen to the tape. Consider whether the dream is telling you anything useful about your feelings or your current situation.

to time provide a direct spur to creativity, as in the case of the interior designer who dreamed she was surrounded by strange colors. On waking, she realized that her dream could be the starting point for an original color scheme.

Symbolic solution

Dreams often provide suggestions for solutions to personal problems. For example, a 35-year-old woman was trying to decide whether she should quit her secure job as a secretary to take a riskier but potentially more fulfilling position in sales. One night the woman dreamed she was on a seashore about to enter the water. At first the ocean seemed full of the shadowy, threatening forms of sharks. But when the animals broke the surface, she realized they were in fact a school of dolphins. She then stepped into the water without hesitation. On waking, she interpreted her dream as meaning that her fears of a career change were exaggerated. She felt encouraged to take the plunge as she had in her dream.

As this example shows, making sense of dreams is itself a creative activity. American psychologist Calvin Hall once described a dream as "a letter to oneself." By learning to read these letters you may discover much about your desires and your fears.

CHAPTER TWO

STYLES OF THINKING

ONE CHARACTERISTIC OF the naturally creative individual is the ability to solve problems in fresh and inventive ways. Often, it is neither high IQ nor technical or scientific grounding that enables a person to find the key to problem solving. Rather it is a certain style of thinking, one that circumvents many of the obstacles that stand in the way of effective solutions.

This chapter will help you find new perspectives on old problems. It also discusses ways to shake off some of the negative, dead-end patterns of thinking that you may have adopted in the past. By working through creative-thinking tests, and by reading how other people have tackled problems at work and at home—everything from inventing the Velcro clothes fastener to repairing a lawnmower—you can gain the confidence to employ a wide variety of fresh thinking techniques.

Many people have heard of Edward de Bono's lateral thinking and, perhaps, read his books or tried some of his peculiar puzzles, but few realize how effective his approach can be when it comes to solving everyday problems. Whether it helps you get rid of an unpopular boss at work or dream up a novel way to ask a favor of a friend, stepping sideways into lateral thinking will inspire a host of creative and practical solutions.

With the help of the other styles of thinking outlined in this chapter, you can, for example, learn how to make the most of randomly generated ideas. You can also start to make connections between areas of thinking that are usually kept separate, or maybe translate into pictures a thorny problem that has hitherto baffled you in words.

Often, what sets effective problem solvers apart from the rest of the population is simply their readiness to devote time to the task at hand. So possibly the greatest aid to creative problem solving is the ability to become completely involved with what you are doing; if you can combine patience and concentration with a range of effective thinking techniques, you may be able to crack even seemingly insoluble conundrums.

THERE IS NO SINGLE KEY TO CREATIVE
THINKING. DIFFERENT STYLES OF THOUGHT WILL
UNLOCK DIFFERENT PROBLEMS.

GRASP THE PROBLEM

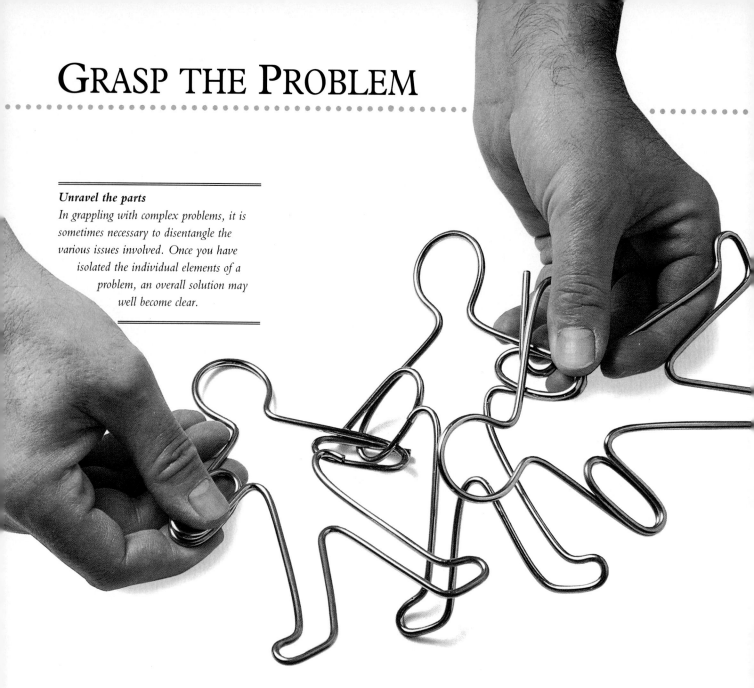

PROBLEM SOLVING IS ONE of the most useful
applications of creative thinking. But to work
out a successful solution to a problem, you must
first be willing to become thoroughly involved
with it. Psychologist Marvin Levine from the State
University of New York at Stony Brook calls this
process of coming to grips with a problem "intimate engagement." He maintains that the extent to
which you are motivated can make a crucial difference in your ability to find creative answers.

According to Levine, two main principles are
involved in this process. First, you must show your
full commitment to the problem by giving it as
much time and energy as you can possibly spare.
Second, you must be ready to examine the task
from every conceivable angle, which means scruti-
nizing it physically and thinking it through.

But how do you engage a problem in this manner?
Take the following puzzle:

$$
\begin{array}{r}
AD \\
+\,DU \\
\hline
DUD
\end{array}
$$

Each of the letters A, U, and D stands for a digit
between zero and nine. If the same digit is always
represented by the same letter, what digit does
each letter stand for?

Never give up
Some people will set to and relish the challenge of
solving a problem like this. Others—often those
with a history of failing at such tasks—will tend to
dismiss it without a second glance, not wishing to
risk disappointment. But don't be too quick to
give up. Put aside your apprehension and engage in

MAN AGAINST MACHINE

Learning to engage yourself intimately with problems can help you resolve practical everyday difficulties—but only if you make the effort to try.

American psychologist Marvin Levine cites the example of his 15-year-old clothes dryer. When the machine suddenly squealed to a stop one day, Levine, who was terrified of tinkering with appliances, at first did not even consider attempting a repair; he resigned himself instead to buying a new dryer. But then he noticed a panel at the back of the machine, which was held in place by four screws. Assuming that the machine was defunct anyway, he decided he would undo it.

What's inside?

Instead of discovering an incomprehensible tangle of machine parts, as he had feared, Levine saw only lint. Over the years, bits of fluff from clothes had built up, clogging the dryer and ultimately bringing it to a halt. Levine vacuumed out the lint, and to his great satisfaction, the dryer once again worked perfectly. It was as simple as that.

Levine uses this example to demonstrate how taking on a new challenge can help you see that you are capable of succeeding. And that in turn can lead you to take on additional challenges in the future. After his revelation with the dryer, Levine was always willing to have a go at repairing other broken appliances, and the results were often gratifying.

But time and application alone will not solve every problem. Difficulty arises when you look at a piece of equipment and cannot immediately understand how it works.

A practical first step in such situations is to locate an object just like the one you want to repair, and then study it to see how it differs from the broken object. A woman whose car seat was stuck, for example, peered under the seat, but could see nothing obviously wrong. She then went around to the passenger seat and looked under it. She noticed it had a spring that was missing from the broken seat. By comparing the two seats, she was able to work out what was needed.

If you cannot locate another example of the object you are fixing, try going to a library or bookstore for information on repairing it. Many how-to books are written with the novice in mind.

Also, remember that the more often you take on such challenging repairs, the better equipped you will be for dealing with such crises in the future. By building your knowledge and skill in a particular problem area, you will increase your ability to solve subsequent challenges creatively. You will also find yourself becoming more confident about taking on such challenges.

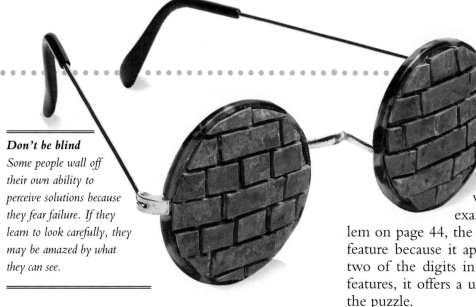

Don't be blind
Some people wall off their own ability to perceive solutions because they fear failure. If they learn to look carefully, they may be amazed by what they can see.

the problem. You will find it is easier than you thought—perhaps even enjoyable.

Write down every little clue about the problem. Here is a hint to start: Although U is added to D in the right-hand column, D remains unchanged. What does this tell you about the value of U? Yet when D is added to A, you get a two-digit answer whose first digit is D. What does this tell you about the value of D? Once you have answered these questions, you will have the problem all but solved. (The solution is on page 136.)

Most problems require effort. The chief difference between people who find solutions and those who don't is that the solvers try harder and don't give up. Readiness to come to grips with a problem—Levine's "intimate engagement"—is an essential ingredient for success.

Question of time
A crucial factor in problem solving is setting aside enough time to tackle the task confronting you. Not surprisingly in this age of instant gratification, many people fail to take this simple fact into consideration. American psychiatrist M. Scott Peck, the author of *The Road Less Traveled,* has described how he suddenly realized time's importance in problem solving when he was complaining to a neighbor one day about his inability to mend mechanical objects. The neighbor, after listening to the psychiatrist's lengthy lament, simply replied, "That's because you don't take the time!" Peck was stunned by the obvious truth in the statement. It became clear to him in a flash that to engage intimately in a problem, he first had to set aside a little time for it.

Apart from taking time and trouble, you can improve your problem solving by applying a few

simple principles. First, look for any special features within the problem that can help you begin to work out a solution. For example, in the arithmetic problem on page 44, the letter D stands out as a special feature because it appears in both columns and as two of the digits in the sum. With these unique features, it offers a useful starting point for solving the puzzle.

Try out this problem-solving principle by finding the special feature in the following problem, and then work out the answer: A couple named Jack and Jill once built a rectangular house on which all of the sides faced south. One day Jill

BREAK THE CHAIN

Try this puzzle to test your problem-solving skills. A young traveler called Dan arrives at a hotel and explains to the manager that he would like to stay there for the next 15 days. He adds that, unfortunately, he has no money or credit cards, but produces a chain of 15 valuable platinum links and offers to pay the manager one link per day.

The manager realizes that the hotel stands to make a sizeable profit from this arrangement, so he agrees to accept the links as payment for Dan's bill provided he is paid every day. The manager points out, however, that a cut link is nowhere near as valuable as one that is intact. He makes it clear that he does not want to end up with 15 cut links at the end of 15 days.

What is the smallest number of links Dan can cut to honor his side of the agreement? (It is perfectly acceptable for the guest and the manager to swap links; for example, on the second day the guest may exchange a string of two links for the one the hotel manager is holding.)

Here is a hint to get you started: Don't attempt to work out the whole problem at once. Simplify it first for a smaller number of days and links. Turn to page 136 for the complete solution.

spotted a bear ambling by their new home. What color was the bear? For this problem, the most useful bit of information is the directional orientation of the house. Where in the world is it possible to have nothing but southern exposures? The only possible answer is the North Pole. The solution to the problem then becomes clear: The bear is white, because it is a polar bear.

Another useful approach to problem solving is to consider the logical limits imposed by a particular situation. Consider the example of two vertical poles, both 10 feet high, that stand at

either end of a clothesline. The line is 15 feet long, strung from the top of one pole to the top of the other. It hangs freely between the poles. The lowest point of the line is 2.5 feet above the ground. The question you have to answer is: How far apart are the poles?

Poles apart

Here the quickest route to a solution is to consider the extremes; how far apart could the poles possibly be? You will see that the maximum is 15 feet. But if this were the case, the line would be taut and 10 feet above the ground.

Now assess the opposite extreme: How close could

THE TOWERS OF HANOI

The Towers of Hanoi puzzle will demonstrate how important it is to break down a problem into manageable parts.

You have three "towers," or poles, marked A, B, and C. There is a pile of rings on pole A, stacked in order of size from the largest at the bottom to the smallest at the top. The task is to move all the rings to pole C, stacking them in the same order. Larger disks can never be placed on top of smaller ones. You can move only one ring at a time, and you must put it on one of the three poles—rings cannot be set temporarily aside.

The way to approach this problem is to start with the simplest version, involving just two rings. The solution is easy: First move the top ring from A to B and the bottom ring to C. Then move the smaller ring to C.

Next, tackle the problem with three rings. You will notice from the two-ring example that before moving the bottom ring to pole C, you must move all the rings above it to B. The correct solution is shown in step-by-step form below, although you may want to try solving it for yourself before you look at the answer.

Now you are ready to try a four-ring version. Again you have to shift all the rings from A to C. Start by moving the smallest disk to B first. The solution is on page 137.

the poles be? The answer, of course, is zero feet, or right next to each other. At this distance the clothesline would be folded in half, 7.5 feet on each side—and its lowest point would be 2.5 feet from the ground. So the poles are zero feet apart. By searching for the longest and shortest possible distances between the poles you were able to deduce the correct answer without becoming bogged down in mathematical calculations.

Simplicity itself

This method of "going to extremes" to solve problems only works for certain types of puzzle. At its core, however, is the guiding principle that lies behind much successful problem solving—simplification. The puzzles "Break the chain" on page 46, "The towers of Hanoi" on the opposite page, and "Counterfeit gold" below provide different examples of how simplification can lead to solutions.

One of the most common forms of simplification is the recognition of subgoals—interim objectives that do not solve the whole problem, but that take you closer to a solution. For example, you will never solve a complex problem like the four-ring version of the towers of Hanoi without recognizing the interim steps you must take along the way.

These techniques—simplification, seeking out special features, and looking for extremes—can help you solve a wide variety of practical problems. Use them to take on a new challenge, whether it be fixing a broken appliance in your house or solving a computer program problem at work. Problem solving can be fun and deeply satisfying, if you have the right attitude. Remember, you must engage the problem intimately and allow yourself enough time to consider all possible approaches. Energy, time, focused attention—these are the primary aids to creative problem solving.

Counterfeit gold

Imagine that you are given 10 piles of 10 gold coins. Each genuine coin weighs two ounces. Unfortunately, one stack is made up entirely of counterfeit coins, each weighing a single ounce. To help you identify the counterfeit stack, you are given a set of kitchen scales. But you are told you can only use the scales once. How can you work out which of the 10 piles is made up of counterfeits in just one weighing? To solve this puzzle, start by simplifying it: Try the problem first with just three stacks of three coins. The answer is on page 137.

LATERAL THINKING

YOUR BRAIN HAS an amazing ability to organize the information it accumulates into sensible, logical patterns. But once information is organized in this way, the patterns become set, and it is often difficult to change them. The patterns can be dislodged, however, with a thought process known as lateral thinking, which can be envisaged as working across your normal paths of logic rather than following along them. According to British psychologist Edward de Bono, who devised the term, lateral thinking can be used by anyone to generate new and excitingly creative ideas.

A fresh angle

The brain uses logical thought patterns to make sense of a highly complex world, and it clings to its well-worn mental tracks tenaciously. Yet, as De Bono recognized, unique and, often, quite simple ideas or solutions to problems are not necessarily the product of logical, or "vertical," thinking. In logical thinking, we are concerned with "what is." But de Bono suggests that really effective creativity requires consciously adopting a thinking approach that helps you step outside the usual boundaries so you can see see "what might be."

When thinking vertically, you extend a thought by logical steps, each one following from the step that preceded it, with all steps moving in a single direction. But, as De Bono points out in his book *Serious Creativity*, "You cannot dig a hole in a different place by digging the same hole deeper." To find a truly different approach, you must think laterally, not vertically, and move sideways.

Work problem solved

In *The Creative Spirit*, authors Daniel Goleman, Paul Kaufman, and Michael Ray give the following example of lateral thinking in practice. A man loves his job and works well with his colleagues, but he consistently fails to get along with his boss. This affects him so badly that he feels he will have to leave his job. Reluctantly, he goes to see an executive headhunter to discuss other options. Then, suddenly, he has a lateral thought: Why not give his boss's résumé to the headhunter? The headhunter finds the boss a better job, which he takes. The man happily remains with his current firm and is eventually promoted to his boss's position.

AN IDEA MAN

Edward de Bono is famous for originating the term "lateral thinking," and for his creative approaches to thinking, which have been used by millions of people throughout the world. Du Pont, American Standard Oil, Exxon, United Technologies, ICI, the government of California, and many others have sought De Bono's advice. According to a top executive at Du Pont, De Bono once saved the company $30 million with a single idea.

De Bono has produced his own offbeat solutions for many of the world's problems. When he was looking for lateral solutions to ecology issues, for example, he came up with the idea of situating factories downstream from the pollution they produce. The polluters would then become the principal recipients of the pollution, and would thus be motivated to do something about it.

He also thought up a new voting system in which everyone would cast two votes—one for the chosen candidate and one against the candidate the voter most dislikes. With this method, De Bono argued, democracy would work more fairly because extremists would be unlikely to get into power.

De Bono today directs a Task Force on Thinking in Washington, D.C. He also runs the world's largest curriculum program for the teaching of thinking in schools, and has written more than 30 books.

BRAINTEASERS

Some of the most famous examples of lateral thinking find expression in brain-teasing riddles. For example: A man goes into a bar, orders a drink, and chats with the waitress. She screams; he thanks her and leaves. What happened? Answer: The man had hiccups and she screamed to cure him with a good scare.

Try the following two problems for yourself. (The answers are on page 137.)

1. You walk into a room and discover Mabel and George lying dead on the floor. The window is open. There is a small pool of water and some broken glass on the floor near the bodies. Who are Mabel and George and how did they die?

2. In the middle of a field on a sunny day, you come across a damp patch of grass, a carrot, an old hat, and a couple of lumps of coal. What has happened?

With lateral thinking, the normal perceptions of a problem can change. In *Serious Creativity*, De Bono gives the example of a three-year-old girl who is always bothering her grandmother. One parent suggests putting the little girl in the playpen to keep her out of mischief. But the other parent comes up with a lateral solution, which is to put the grandmother into the playpen to keep her out of the little girl's way!

The way you perceive a problem has a vital effect on your ability to devise a suitable solution. De Bono uses the example of a young boy in Australia whose friend offers him the choice between a large $1 coin and a smaller $2 coin. The boy invariably picks the larger $1 coin, which leads his friends to assume that he is stupid for not realizing that the smaller coin is more valuable.

What seems odd is that the boy never recognizes his mistake. Every time he is offered a choice between the coins, he goes for the bigger, less valuable one. One day, an adult observes this scene and tries to point out to the little boy that he is losing out by taking the larger coin. But, the little boy retorts, how many times would his friends

have offered him the choice if he had taken the $2 coin the first time?

Thinking about the problem in a lateral way, he had assessed how his friends were likely to behave if he took the $1 coin. He had decided that if he took the risk of pretending that he did not understand the joke, the choice would be presented to him more than twice. Logic alone dictated that he take the $2 coin, but this boy's lateral solution earned him a great deal of money!

Change of focus
Lateral thinking certainly doesn't hold the solution to every kind of problem. Many problems demand logical, vertical thinking. The idea of concentrated laundry detergent, for example, was the logical solution to the problem of laundry detergent requiring too much space on supermarket shelves. First, the problem was isolated: Large detergent containers are hard to display, heavy to carry, and expensive to transport. Then, using logical, vertical reasoning, the problem was solved: By making detergent more concentrated, it could be packaged in smaller, lighter, and less expensive containers.

FOUR KNIVES, THREE BOTTLES, AND A TUMBLER

In *The 5-Day Course in Thinking*, Edward de Bono presents the following challenge: You have three bottles, four knives with flat handles, and a tumbler filled with water. Can you make a platform to support the tumbler using knives and just one bottle? Can you do it using two bottles? All three bottles?

Solution 1. This approach uses all of the knives, but just one bottle. The knife blades are interlocked to make a stable platform, and the weight of the tumbler holds it firmly on top of the bottle.

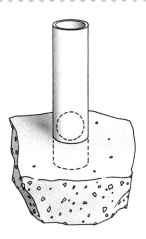

Retrieve the ball

A steel pipe about six inches long is embedded in a concrete floor, and a table tennis ball is lying at the bottom of the pipe. You have 100 feet of clothesline, a bowl of breakfast cereal, a pitcher of milk, a screwdriver, a wire coat hanger, a wrench, and a light bulb. How many ways can you devise to get the ball out of the pipe without damaging the ball, the pipe, or the floor? *Turn to page 138 for the answers.*

Solution 2. This platform is made using all three bottles and just three knives. The slight flexibility of the knife blades can be exploited to make them interlock.

Solution 3. The interlocking of the knife blades allows one of the bottles to be removed, and the weight of the knife handles will balance the glass of water.

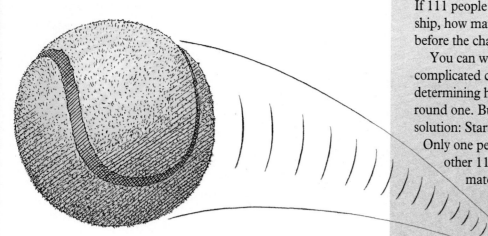

If 111 people enter a tennis singles championship, how many matches will have to be played before the champion is decided?

You can work out the answer by making complicated calculations on paper, beginning by determining how many seeded players bypass round one. But there is a much easier route to a solution: Start with the result and work backward. Only one person will win the championship; the other 110 will lose. So, with one loser per match, a total of 110 matches is needed. Coming at the problem from an unusual angle gives a simple solution.

Lateral thinking comes into its own when an original invention or a completely new idea is required to solve a problem—particularly in new or little-understood fields. De Bono cites the example of the manufacturers Black and Decker, who were so focused on the development of power tools that they neglected to considered where such tools are used. An enterprising inventor who set his mind to this problem came up with the "workmate," a wood-and-metal foldaway workbench that holds tools and has clamps for securing materials. It is strong, simple, and maneuverable, and Black and Decker—which eventually bought the invention—has sold millions of them. Yet no one had thought to invent such a device because no one had ever focused on the right question.

Try provocation
De Bono suggests that creative solutions can be deliberately or spontaneously provoked by statements that, on the surface, seem absurd. In other words, a ridiculous or impractical idea can lead to a sensible and effective solution.

As an example, he cites the case of a man who wrote to the British Ministry of Defence during the 1930s, suggesting that the British government consider making a radio wave capable of shooting down aircraft. The head of the ministry rejected the idea as absurd, but his assistant thought about it, turned it around, and suggested that the reflection of a radio wave might be useful in detecting aircraft. From what appeared to be a ridiculous suggestion, the concept of radar was born.

You can use several techniques to deliberately provoke lateral thinking. One technique involves purposely setting aside all preconceived notions about an object or situation. To demonstrate how people need to open their minds to new ways of looking at things, De Bono asks them to think about a cup for drinking tea. Most people visualize the traditional circular cup with a handle, and an accompanying saucer. But when he asks them to throw away their preconceived notions about the cup, De Bono provokes a surprisingly wide range of fresh mental images. People begin to create cups without handles, or ones without saucers, or ones that are square or triangular.

Negative into positive
One way to stop taking things for granted is to begin with an obviously false assessment of the situation. A few years ago, for example, people might have said "cars run on gas." To provoke thought, you could say "cars do *not* run on gas." What could they be made to run on instead? Water? Electricity? Methane? Solar power? Sugar by-products? All of these would have seemed absurd, but scientists now recognize their practicality. Indeed, some of them are in use. This kind of lateral thinking opens up a variety of possibilities.

De Bono suggests that, when working in groups, it can be helpful to preface a provocative statement with the nonsense word *po*. For example, "*Po*, the

office could hold another six people." The word *po* indicates that what you are about to say may sound absurd and will not be logical. It is a quick way of saying "this may not make any sense but..." or "what if?"

Of course, for this to work effectively the people you are talking to must also be aware of the technique of provocation! Saying *po* might seem artificial and embarrassing at first, but provoking new ideas by taking seemingly outlandish positions on issues can be very useful.

African letter trick

The main appeal of lateral thinking lies in its ingenuity. It offers a way of solving problems that is not only effective but also often fun. The enjoyment comes from devising truly clever solutions. Here is one more amusing example.

An American Peace Corps worker in Africa used lateral thinking one day to solve a transportation problem. He lived in a tiny village, miles from the nearest small town. One market day, he took his car to the town for repairs.

The mechanic told him it wouldn't be ready until the next day. A bus ran between the man's village and the town—but only once a week, on market day. The man could take the bus back to his village that day, but he would have to find another form of transportation in order to pick up his car. The bus would not be running the next day, and his rural neighbors had no way of helping him get to town.

What was the solution? The man recalled that the postman always made a detour to call at the village on those rare occasions when there was a letter to deliver. Few people in the village could read, so very little mail was received. Before leaving the town, the Peace Corps worker posted a letter to his village, addressed to himself. When the mail van arrived at his home the next day to deliver the letter, the man hitched a ride back to town and collected his car.

Cube teaser

The cube at right has been made in two halves joined with dovetail joints on all four sides. Although it looks impossible to separate the two halves, in fact they come apart easily. Can you work out how the cube is designed to make this possible? The solution can be found on page 138.

AVOID FUNCTIONAL FIXITY

I F YOU WANT TO EXCEL at creative problem solving, you have to strive for maximum mental flexibility. A common trap to avoid, first highlighted by German psychologist Karl Duncker during the 1930s, is the inflexible belief that familiar objects can only have one purpose.

Duncker postulated that all thought is limited by experience, so that as we learn how things work—from machines to social interactions—their functions become fixed in our minds and we are unable to imagine them being used in any other way. For example, a box is a container, a hammer is used for knocking in nails, and a tire must always be put on a wheel. Duncker called this unimaginative use of objects "functional fixity" and recognized it as a major impediment to creativity.

The missing hammer

In one of his experiments, Duncker asked individual students to perform the simple task of hanging a pendulum on the wall. He placed a nail and a cord with a pendulum weight attached to its end on a table, along with some miscellaneous objects. All the students had to do was drive the nail into the wall and hang the pendulum from it. But no hammer had been supplied. Only 50 percent of the students discovered the obvious solution—using the pendulum as a hammer.

The difficulty the students had in solving this problem makes it clear how stubborn the mind can become in clinging to fixed ways of doing things. To half the students involved in Duncker's experiment, the pendulum had only one purpose.

Take a brick

Of course, it takes time and practice to learn to think in a flexible manner and to gain what psychologists call "functional freedom." Start by trying to imagine ways in which you could use a simple brick, other than as a building material. For example, you could heat the brick in an oven, wrap it in

Tire tricks

An old tire can be recycled in any number of useful or entertaining ways. With a little creative thought, you can reuse valuable raw materials and reduce waste.

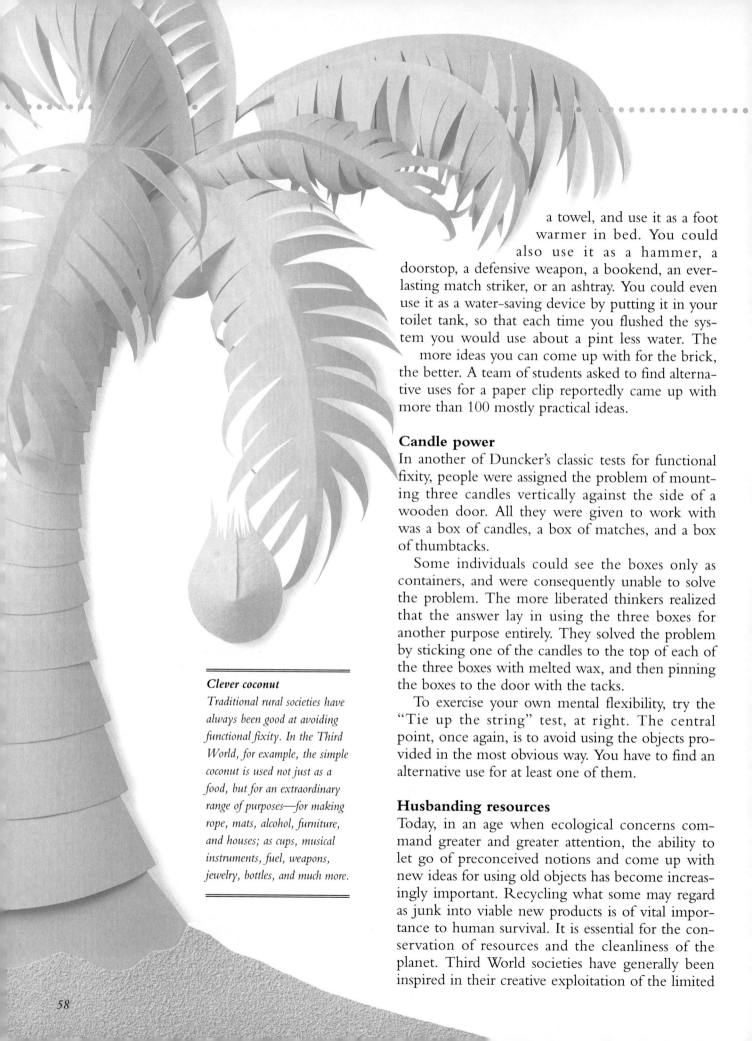

a towel, and use it as a foot warmer in bed. You could also use it as a hammer, a doorstop, a defensive weapon, a bookend, an everlasting match striker, or an ashtray. You could even use it as a water-saving device by putting it in your toilet tank, so that each time you flushed the system you would use about a pint less water. The more ideas you can come up with for the brick, the better. A team of students asked to find alternative uses for a paper clip reportedly came up with more than 100 mostly practical ideas.

Candle power

In another of Duncker's classic tests for functional fixity, people were assigned the problem of mounting three candles vertically against the side of a wooden door. All they were given to work with was a box of candles, a box of matches, and a box of thumbtacks.

Some individuals could see the boxes only as containers, and were consequently unable to solve the problem. The more liberated thinkers realized that the answer lay in using the three boxes for another purpose entirely. They solved the problem by sticking one of the candles to the top of each of the three boxes with melted wax, and then pinning the boxes to the door with the tacks.

To exercise your own mental flexibility, try the "Tie up the string" test, at right. The central point, once again, is to avoid using the objects provided in the most obvious way. You have to find an alternative use for at least one of them.

Husbanding resources

Today, in an age when ecological concerns command greater and greater attention, the ability to let go of preconceived notions and come up with new ideas for using old objects has become increasingly important. Recycling what some may regard as junk into viable new products is of vital importance to human survival. It is essential for the conservation of resources and the cleanliness of the planet. Third World societies have generally been inspired in their creative exploitation of the limited

Clever coconut

Traditional rural societies have always been good at avoiding functional fixity. In the Third World, for example, the simple coconut is used not just as a food, but for an extraordinary range of purposes—for making rope, mats, alcohol, furniture, and houses; as cups, musical instruments, fuel, weapons, jewelry, bottles, and much more.

Tie up the string

Two strings are attached to the ceiling in the picture at right; the test is to tie their ends together. Unfortunately they are too far apart to allow you to reach one while holding the other. Imagine that you have a pair of scissors, a hammer, and a clothes peg at your disposal. Using one or more of these objects, it is possible to tie the strings together. Remember, you can use any or all of the objects in an unusual manner. The solution is on page 138.

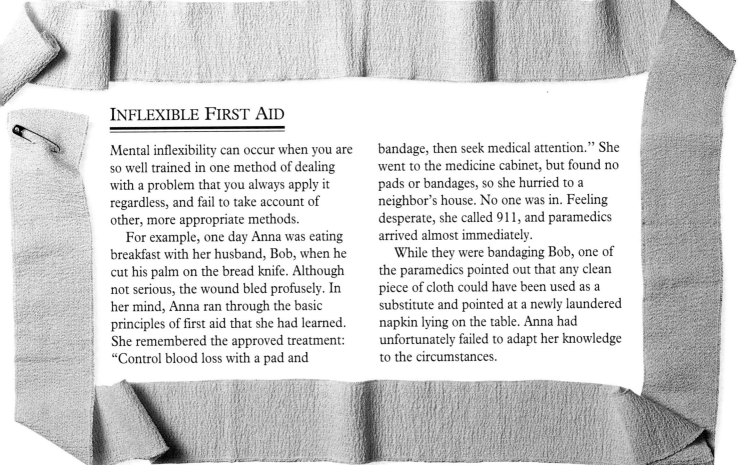

INFLEXIBLE FIRST AID

Mental inflexibility can occur when you are so well trained in one method of dealing with a problem that you always apply it regardless, and fail to take account of other, more appropriate methods.

For example, one day Anna was eating breakfast with her husband, Bob, when he cut his palm on the bread knife. Although not serious, the wound bled profusely. In her mind, Anna ran through the basic principles of first aid that she had learned. She remembered the approved treatment: "Control blood loss with a pad and bandage, then seek medical attention." She went to the medicine cabinet, but found no pads or bandages, so she hurried to a neighbor's house. No one was in. Feeling desperate, she called 911, and paramedics arrived almost immediately.

While they were bandaging Bob, one of the paramedics pointed out that any clean piece of cloth could have been used as a substitute and pointed at a newly laundered napkin lying on the table. Anna had unfortunately failed to adapt her knowledge to the circumstances.

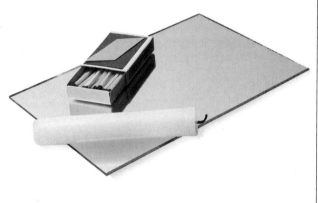

SECRET MESSAGE

Imagine you are a spy being held in solitary confinement by foreign terrorists. Once a day you are visited by a sympathetic guard. He cannot speak your language, but he has indicated through sign language that he will take a message to an outside contact who is waiting faithfully for you at an appointed place.

However, except for a primitive bed, your cell contains only a box of matches, a candle, and a hand mirror. How can you write an SOS message to your contact using only these items?

To discover several possible alternative ways in which you could have written the message, turn to page 138.

resources available to them. The Indonesians have a saying, for example, that there are as many uses for a coconut as days in the year. Convincing the people of advanced industrial countries to show the same ingenuity with their everyday resources—from soft drink cans to old car tires—is an elusive goal.

Tried and tested

The failure to use an object for more than a single fixed purpose is only one example of mental inflexibility. Another is the unwillingness to depart from a prearranged plan or a tried and true method. If a procedure has been found to work once, most people will use it over and over again, even though circumstances change and better solutions become available. As the weeks pass, for example, you might find that you always use the same route to visit a friend's home, even though it may not be the shortest or quickest way. It just happens to be the route you discovered the first time you paid a visit, so you stick to it.

This kind of unexamined routine has been called "satisficing"—being satisfied with a second-rate solution because, after all, it does get you there in the end. People prone to such mental laziness will tend to argue against change on the grounds that "they've always done it that way." The creative approach, by contrast, involves always being open to the possibility of fresh solutions, believing that there must be better ways of doing things, and trying to find them.

Psychologist Abraham Luchins's water jar puzzle, which you can try for yourself at right, is a test of your readiness to adopt fresh procedures in changing circumstances. To solve this complex problem

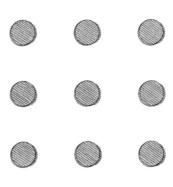

most efficiently, you have to work out a formula, apply it for a while—and then abandon it. Unless you are already a skilled practitioner of this type of thinking, you probably will not be able to detect the alternative—and easier—formula which applies to some of the later examples in this test. One psychologist calculated that up to 75 percent of people fail to see the simple solution because they have already set their minds on the first formula and are blind to the possibility of an alternative.

Seeing new possibilities in an object or exploring fresh solutions to problems comes much more naturally to some people than others. It is an area in which anyone can improve, however. By freeing yourself from old mental habits and the self-created boundaries that limit your thinking, you will be able to see problems in a new light.

Join the dots

In this test, you have to connect all nine dots using four straight lines and without lifting your pencil from the page. When you have done the four-line test, try to join the dots using three straight lines. Finally, can you connect them with only one line? The solutions are on pages 138 and 139.

THE WATER JAR TEST

Imagine you have three jars, A, B, and C. All are different shapes and none have measurements indicated on them. Given that jar A holds 11 fluidounces of water, that jar B holds 9 fluidounces, and that jar C holds 4 fluidounces, how can you measure out 6 fluidounces using the three jugs?

The answer: Fill up the 11 fluidounce jar, A. Then pour as much water into jug B as it will hold. Since B holds 9 fluidounces, A will have 2 left. Now

fill jar C and pour the contents, which you know to be 4, into jar A to get 6 fluidounces. To measure out the specified amount of water, you had to follow the sequence: A into B, C into A.

Now work out the sequence of moves that will solve problems 2 through 8, below. In each case, you know only the capacity of the jars and the amount of water to measure. The sequence need not always be the same. The answers are on page 139.

	Capacity of jars (fluidounces)			Desired amount of water
	A	**B**	**C**	
1 (example)	11	9	4	6
2	15	90	4	67
3	14	163	25	99
4	18	43	10	5
5	9	42	6	21
6	20	59	4	31
7	14	36	8	6
8	23	49	3	20

GIVE CHANCE A CHANCE

SERENDIPITY, OR THE HAPPY ability to find valuable things, such as the answer to a problem, by pure chance, has played a major role in many notable inventions and discoveries. In 1781, for instance, the Abbé René Haüy, a French university professor and amateur geologist, discovered the laws of crystallization when he dropped and shattered a friend's prized calcite crystal. Despite his embarrassment, the abbé was fascinated to see that the crystal had broken into different, but equally perfect, geometric forms. After smashing crystals in his own collection and studying the results, the abbé formulated a set of rules that accurately described the geometric structure of crystals.

The great inventor Thomas Edison also benefited from serendipity. He was partially deaf and at one point he was having trouble deciphering Morse code telephone messages, so he created a repeater device that recorded the dots and dashes on wax. This allowed him to play messages back at his leisure. While trying to eliminate the rattling noises of the lever that recorded the code, Edison accidentally speeded up the repeater and noticed that it produced speechlike sounds. Instead of automatically silencing these noises, he came up with the idea of enhancing them. The historic result was the invention of the phonograph in 1877.

Harnessing chance

"The history of discovery is full of such arrivals at unexpected destinations," observed the Hungarian-born philosopher Arthur Koestler, "and arrivals at the right destination by the wrong boat." Recognizing the often dazzling effect of chance in opening up new angles to an alert mind, many experimenters have looked for ways to harness randomness into some sort of system, so as to give creative thinking a push. Naturally, you can't expect to find the cure for a fatal illness if you don't have a background in medical research. Nor is it likely that you will compose a great symphony without a thorough grounding in music. But by using some simple techniques you can begin to deploy the power of chance to stimulate your own originality and inventiveness.

Limber up your imagination

One approach involves freeing your imagination from conscious control. Over the years, many people working in literature and the arts have sought to enhance their creativity through a variety of such methods. French poet and artist André Breton apparently found random doodling a sure source of inspiration, while the Irish poet William Butler Yeats recommended automatic writing—a technique that he believed allowed him to record his unconscious thoughts.

To try a version of automatic writing yourself, begin by scribbling down the first words that come into your head. After five minutes, look at what you have produced and attempt to apply the ideas that sprang to mind to the problem that is preoccupying you. You may also be able to use those ideas as a starting point for a more coherent piece of writing. While such spontaneous thoughts are never completely random, this practice tends to loosen your conscious control over ideas and can lead to a wide range of creative insights.

Hitcher's guide

A more dramatic way to break out of mental ruts is to hitch ideas on a random prop. For example, imagine that you are in financial difficulty and need to find ways to economize. Try closing your eyes, turning around, then opening them again; do this in several parts of your house and write down the first 10 things you see. Now let your imagination expand to discover ways to save money. Looking at a houseplant, for instance, might suggest digging up the backyard and planting vegetables, so as to reduce your food bills. Another imaginative approach is to make a list of

Random creation

Do you see the rabbit in the ink spill? Accidents can stimulate the imagination and provide keys to creative problem solving—if you can recognize the hidden possibilities.

A WINNING COMBINATION

The discovery of penicillin by Scottish bacteriologist Alexander Fleming is another celebrated example of how a chance event, interpreted by an inventive mind, led to an important scientific breakthrough.

In the summer of 1920, before going off on vacation, Fleming set out some uncovered culture plates in which he was growing bacteria. While he was gone, a spore of mold blew in the window and landed in one of the plates. On his return, Fleming noticed a bacteria-free circle around the bit of mold on the plate. Intrigued, he tested the mold and found it to be of a type called *Penicillium*. He realized that a chemical in the mold had killed the bacteria; he named the chemical penicillin. Eventually, Fleming's insight and the work of several other scientists led to the manufacture of a drug that became a formidable weapon against disease.

In 1945, Fleming and two others got the Nobel Prize for this discovery—a breakthrough that resulted from pure chance combined with special knowledge and creative thinking.

the first five different occupations that come into your head. Then pretend that you are skilled in each of them in turn, and ask yourself what economies you could make: "I am a plumber, and I redesign the heating system to function more efficiently; I am a banker, and I renegotiate the terms of my mortgage." Somewhere there are probably practical ideas that you can enact for real.

Pick a word
Another way to inject an element of chance into your thinking is to let a randomly selected word or phrase guide your problem solving. Imagine that you are completely at a loss in deciding what to do with your evening. Find a dictionary and open it at random; shut your eyes and use your finger to select a word. Of course, it is unlikely that this word will relate directly to your predicament. "Myogenic," for instance, seems unpromising at

first. But when you see that it means "originating or forming muscle tissue," you might read a clear message and head for the gym!

Such a "dictionary dive" may not work on the first try, but you can simply try again if the first word is unevocative. Choosing words at random, or any other chance technique, is not a substitute for sound judgment. The idea is to use words as a stimulus to thought—like a stone cast into a pond. You want to break up mental inertia and get ideas flowing. This trick can also be applied to problems more complex than planning an evening. Try it whenever you feel really stymied.

COINING CHANCE

Tossing a coin is the crudest form of random decision making. Approached creatively, however, it can become a method of getting in touch with your real feelings about the choices you face.

For example, Michael couldn't decide whether to vacation in New York or to go to California. He decided to flip a coin. Heads, he would go to California, and tails, he would choose New York.

The first time he tried it, the coin landed tails up. But instead of accepting this chance decision, he simply noted his reaction. He didn't feel good about the plan and resolved to try for two out of three. The second time, the coin showed tails again. Michael noted that his reaction was still negative and realized that he wasn't keen on a trip to New York. He had been working very hard, and the idea of rushing around a crowded city had lost its appeal.

On the final flick of the coin, it landed heads up. Michael felt quite pleased at the thought of relaxing on the beach. As a result, he booked a trip to California, certain he had made the right choice. Flipping a coin, while not making the decision for him, had allowed him to test his feelings about the two options. Faced with your own decisions, you can apply the same technique.

Some other chance techniques are designed to combine ideas at random. Fritz Zwicky, noted astrophysicist at the California Institute of Technology, proposed a method that would enable you to come up with inventions simply by listing the physical properties of objects. To follow Zwicky's approach (which he called "morphological analysis"), you first select a topic to consider, then list the ways in which it might vary. Zwicky recommended that the would-be inventor limit the number of variables to three. If the chosen problem is to find a different type of mobile home, you might consider its shape, the building materials, and the ways in which it could be moved. Once you have made lists for all three variables, pick out a single trait from each list at random. Such blind selection might result in a mobile home of irregular shape, made of fabric, and transported by human energy—a tent!

While three factors are the most manageable number to deal with, there is no limit on how many you could choose to consider—and ingenuity alone will limit the number of possibilities for each category that you devise.

Dictionary dive

Close your eyes, dive into your dictionary, and pick out any word at random. Trying to relate this chance word to a specific problem may uncover possibilities that would otherwise remain hidden.

Inventors start here

Building on Zwicky's idea, two other Americans, architect Don Koberg and graphic designer Jim Bagnall, wrote *The Universal Traveler*, which argues that people do not have to be experts to become inventors. Since many important inventions are improvements on objects that already exist, Koberg and Bagnall recommend that you begin with a

A NEW MODE OF TRANSPORTATION

Put morphological analysis into practice by inventing a novel form of transportation. Imagine you are trying to devise a simple vehicle that will serve as a replacement for the traditional donkey in developing countries. It must carry one person and a small load for considerable distances.

The three variables of the vehicle are its energy or power source, the method of mobility, and the material to be used in its construction. Below is a list of suggestions for each variable.

To invent a vehicle, take one suggestion at random from each of the lists, then put the three together to see what the chance combination produces. In the example below, solar power is the energy source, wood is the material, and caterpillar tracks are the method of mobility. The end result might be a light but sturdy tanklike structure, equipped with a solar panel and capable of traveling over rough terrain. If you had combined skis, wood, and wind, on the other hand, you might have invented a type of "sand-surfer," complete with mast and sail. Invent your own combinations. Some ideas will doubtless be impractical, but others might just be winners.

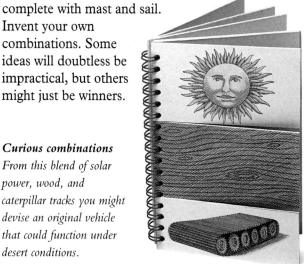

Curious combinations
From this blend of solar power, wood, and caterpillar tracks you might devise an original vehicle that could function under desert conditions.

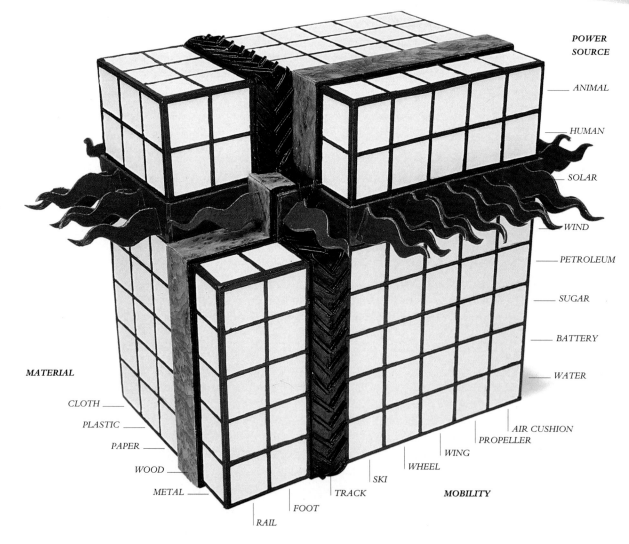

POWER SOURCE
— ANIMAL
— HUMAN
— SOLAR
— WIND
— PETROLEUM
— SUGAR
— BATTERY
— WATER

MOBILITY
AIR CUSHION
PROPELLER
WING
WHEEL
SKI
TRACK
FOOT
RAIL

MATERIAL
CLOTH
PLASTIC
PAPER
WOOD
METAL

device that you believe you could make better in some way—a fountain pen, for example. Start with all the physical attributes of "pen-ness"—the shape, the material, whether or not the pen has a separate cap, what kind of nib it has, and so on. Now list all the options you can imagine for each attribute, no matter how odd they may seem.

What other shapes can pens have?—Square? Faceted? What materials can they be made from?—Wood? Plastic? Cardboard? What can be used to make pen points?—Glass? Ceramic?

When you have written down all the alternatives you can imagine, pick one at random from each list. You might come up with a disposable cardboard pen with a ceramic nib—a not-so-crazy (and possibly even marketable) concept that proves the random selection process can, on occasion, lead to practical ideas.

Analyze what is needed
In his book *Conceptual Blockbusting*, Stanford University's James Adams suggests another approach to inventions. If you want to think up something useful, he proposes, make a list of deficiencies you have noticed around you—such as the lack of left-handed can openers, or of tools for reaching back zippers. Adams suggests that you devote no more than 10 minutes to this exercise

In composing your list, you will automatically begin dreaming up possible ways to meet these needs. Choose a few problems that particularly appeal to you, and—using Zwicky's method—work up lists of solutions for them.

Once again, be sure to include everything that occurs to you, even if it seems ridiculous. Remember, many a practical idea first struck people as bizarre. In some cases, the solution will require that you design new objects. If so, you now know how to analyze an object's physical characteristics to help spur your imagination.

All these random methods will encourage your thoughts to flow more freely in pursuit of creative solutions to practical problems. List making will help you analyze the problems thoroughly, while random selection can give rise to new ideas. Always aim to include all possibilities and avoid censoring your thoughts. That way you will give chance every opportunity to help you.

CALCULATING THE BENEFITS

Once you have generated a few ideas using random thinking methods, you will want to evaluate their merits. Creativity theorist Edward de Bono (see pages 50 to 55), suggests using the Plus-Minus-Interest equation, or PMI—a system for "cost-benefit" analysis.

As a first step, list the P or "plus" factors—the obvious benefits of your invention. Then proceed to the M or "minus" factors, listing all the anticipated costs. Finally, list I or "interesting" factors—all the wider implications, good and bad, of the invention's use and manufacture. Here, include features that are not yet fully worked out. This should help clarify your thoughts. But if you want to be more specific, take the equation one step further by assigning numerical ratings to each feature. Rate them from one to 10.

What price nuclear power?
For example, imagine you are an American scientist analyzing the significance of nuclear development in the 1990s. Your PMI equation and numerical ratings might look like this:

P
Influence of nuclear arms on the worldwide
    balance of power (+5)
An inexhaustible source of energy (+8)
End of carbon-fuel air pollution (+8)

M
Cost of arms race (-8)
Cost of building power stations (-2)
Cost and problems of nuclear
    waste disposal (-5)
Potential nuclear accidents (-8)
Danger of nuclear war (-8)

I
Future uses for nuclear power (+3)
Eventual depletion of world's petroleum (+4)
Construction of safe power stations (+3)
Political change that could bring an end to the
    possibility of nuclear war (+1)

Computing 21(P) - 31(M) +11(I) yields 1, proving the issue of nuclear power to be a delicate balance, but showing how the PMI equation can focus your thoughts about an idea.

INVENTIVE CONNECTIONS

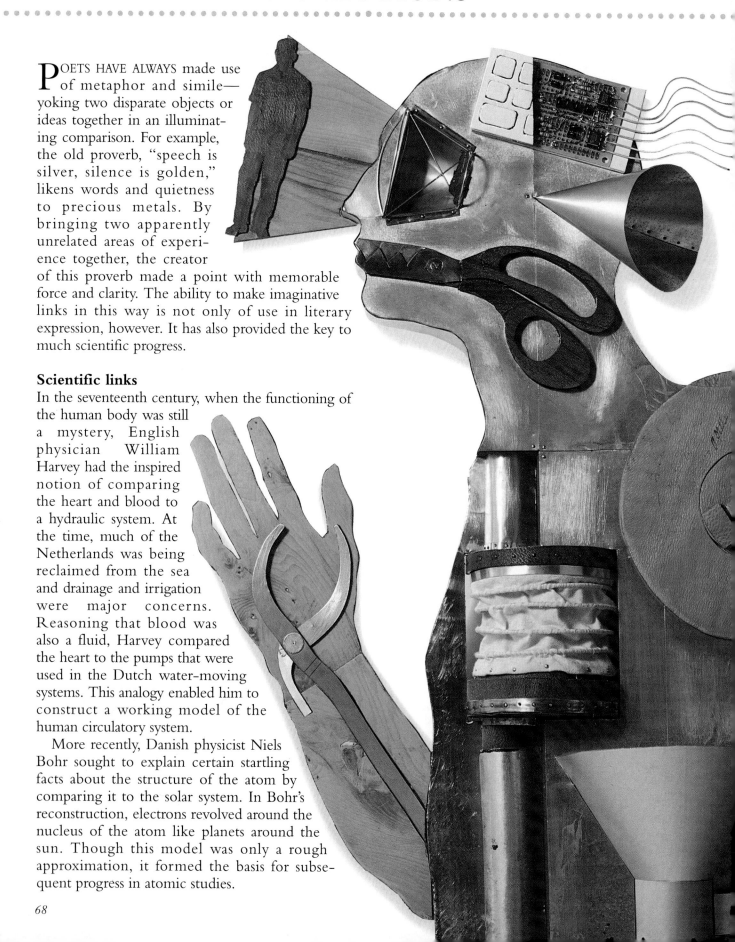

POETS HAVE ALWAYS made use of metaphor and simile—yoking two disparate objects or ideas together in an illuminating comparison. For example, the old proverb, "speech is silver, silence is golden," likens words and quietness to precious metals. By bringing two apparently unrelated areas of experience together, the creator of this proverb made a point with memorable force and clarity. The ability to make imaginative links in this way is not only of use in literary expression, however. It has also provided the key to much scientific progress.

Scientific links

In the seventeenth century, when the functioning of the human body was still a mystery, English physician William Harvey had the inspired notion of comparing the heart and blood to a hydraulic system. At the time, much of the Netherlands was being reclaimed from the sea and drainage and irrigation were major concerns. Reasoning that blood was also a fluid, Harvey compared the heart to the pumps that were used in the Dutch water-moving systems. This analogy enabled him to construct a working model of the human circulatory system.

More recently, Danish physicist Niels Bohr sought to explain certain startling facts about the structure of the atom by comparing it to the solar system. In Bohr's reconstruction, electrons revolved around the nucleus of the atom like planets around the sun. Though this model was only a rough approximation, it formed the basis for subsequent progress in atomic studies.

HOOKS FOR THOUGHT

Velcro, the revolutionary fastener, was created by a Swiss inventor named George de Mestral in 1951. The product was so successful that within six years De Mestral owned his own factory.

The inventor came across his idea after a hunting trip, when he noticed that his clothes were covered with burdock burrs, which proved very difficult to remove. On closer inspection he saw that the burrs owed their sticky nature to a covering of tiny hooklike bristles that could be stuck to his clothes time and again without damaging them.

These bristles gave De Mestral the inspiration for Velcro. The fastener consists of two strips of nylon. The tiny hooks on one strip stick to a coarse surface on the other to form a strong bond, but one that

can be repeatedly broken and remade.

This invention neatly illustrates the phenomenon of cross-fertilization: An observation in one area of life—an ingenious method of plant propagation—provided inspiration for a useful and highly commercial innovation in a purely human sphere. It also shows the importance of careful observation and the potential for such fruitful watchfulness to supply the kind of key insights that set creative minds in motion.

Inventors have also exploited the power of metaphor to connect the previously unconnected. The flexible joints of a desk lamp called an Anglepoise, for example, developed by a British company in the 1930s, were modeled on those of the human arm.

Philosopher and writer Arthur Koestler suggested that the ability to see new connections between different areas of experience or fields of thought was the essence of creativity. In his book *The Act of Creation,* he called it "bisociation," the ability to see "an analogy where no one saw one before." Others have called this process cross-fertilization.

Johannes Gutenberg's invention of the printing press in Germany in the fifteenth

Unusual comparisons
The human body has been a fertile source of inspiration when it comes to creative metaphors. Just as William Harvey likened the heart to a water pump, so others have made such diverse links as the eye with a camera lens, or the brain with a computer.

century provides a perfect demonstration of bisociation in action. As the story goes, Gutenberg developed a method for printing single letters using seals, or primitive bits of type, but he could not work out how to press several seals at once. One day at a wine festival he saw a wine press in action. He realized that the large flat surface of the press could be used to apply many letter seals simultaneously. Once he had connected these two unrelated ideas, the printing press was born.

Daring combinations

Like all thinking techniques, that of making new connections can be learned. The most important thing is preparation, and a vital step in that direction is accumulating a wide range of experience; the specialist may lack the diverse information needed to make unusual combinations.

Creativity benefits from wide reading, alert observation, and a general curiosity about the world. As the story of Velcro shows (see "Hooks for thought" above), nothing is irrelevant to the creative thinker. Whenever you are reading on any subject, ask yourself if what you are learning could apply to other areas that concern you. If, for example, you admire the lavish photographs in a cookbook you use, and you are thinking of redecorating your home, consider how you might use the colors in the photographs to enhance your decor.

A well-trained memory can also be a boon to creativity, since the more of your reading, observation, and experience that is freely available to

you through memory, the more elements your mind will have in play as it searches for new and unusual connections.

But to use your experiences and your powers of recall, you have to take time to practice. People interested in creative writing, for example, can find endless opportunities for exercising their ability to discern new connections. Take an everyday experience—such as traveling to work—and describe it in terms of a single metaphor. Try thinking of the journey as a dangerous river trip during which parked cars become basking alligators, intersections turn into treacherous rapids, and bikes represent fast-moving and potentially hostile canoes.

The personal touch

There are ample opportunities for nonwriters as well to practice metaphorical thinking. Imagine, for instance, that you want to design a personal Christmas card. Christmas is the fixed element— with all its associations of decorated trees, reindeer, snow, and so on. You need to mix this imagery with input from another field of knowledge to lift your card from the realm of cliché.

If you are an art lover, for example, you might employ one of Vincent van Gogh's famous self-portraits, but show the artist in a Santa Claus hood; or you could have one of Paul Gaugin's islanders carry a Christmas turkey instead of a dish of exotic fruit. If you are a scientist, you might show Galileo dropping a Christmas pudding and a feather from the leaning tower of Pisa, recalling his famous gravity experiment with a cannonball. Or you might show venerable Isaac Newton discovering the laws of gravity under a Christmas tree as he is hit on the head by a falling decoration.

Your first attempts at cross-fertilization may seem unproductive or silly. Don't be discouraged. Make your connections one at a time and take heart from the words of artist Louis Danz: "There is nothing mysterious about originality. Nothing fantastic. Originality is merely the step beyond."

SEARCH FOR THE SYMBOL

Graphic symbols are an example of the mind's metaphorical power. The bald eagle, symbol of the United States, represents qualities of nobility and fierceness. Savings institutions are sometimes represented by an acorn, which connotes slow but steady growth. Look at the examples here, then test your ability to cross-fertilize ideas by inventing corporate symbols for each of the following:

Trucking company
Airline
Dry cleaner
Health club

Turn to page 139 for potential solutions.

Night owl
A wise, vigilant, nocturnal animal, the owl, would provide a suitably reassuring corporate image for a firm offering security devices.

Busy collector
Because of the way a squirrel industriously gathers and stores food, it could aptly represent a storage company.

Hunting trophy
A stag could represent a gunsmith. It portrays the outdoor lifestyle and power of the huntsman.

Speedy hare
The corporate image for a delivery service could be a swift and agile hare.

PICTURE THE SOLUTION

ONFRONTED BY A PROBLEM, most people will think about it in words or, if the situation demands, look for a mathematical solution. But the mind also functions on a visual level, and this capacity can be a potent tool in problem solving.

Some problems clearly require visual imagination, which is centered in the right brain (see "Whole-brain thinking" on page 24). If you are trying to work out a more exciting color scheme for your living room, for example, you need to visualize the effect of different color combinations in the drapes, carpets, wallpaper, and furnishings.

But visualization can also help in solving more abstract problems. An outstanding example was provided by physicist Albert Einstein, who frequently used visual thinking to help himself navigate a theoretical plane that defied common sense. In one particularly notable instance, Einstein had what he later called his "happiest thought," an idea that was to provide a key to his far-reaching general theory of relativity.

Visionary answer

In his imagination, Einstein saw a man falling from the roof of a house. He then visualized an object being dropped from the roof at the same time. He could see that, from the point of view of the falling person, the object would not be descending—it would not even seem to be moving. From this, Einstein developed the provocative idea that the person and the object were both in motion and still simultaneously, depending on the observer's viewpoint. This image enabled him to grasp a concept that almost defied logic—time and space are not absolute, but relative.

The use of visualization is by no means restricted to geniuses. Mental imagery is used regularly by expert players of games such as chess or go, for example. They often possess the ability to "see" what the arrangement of pieces on the board will look like after a series of future moves. This form of visual thinking involves the imaginary movement of objects in space, a capacity tested in the exercises on page 75.

Experiments have shown that visualization aids comprehension and

Seeing the problem
Creating pictures in your mind enables you to work out answers to both practical and abstract problems.

memory. In 1973 psychologist Joel R. Levin conducted a study in which he asked one group of children to read a 12-sentence story. A second group was given the same story but told to think of a picture for each sentence. The group that was encouraged to visualize recalled much more information; similar experiments with adults yielded comparable results.

Missing imagery

To see how visualization improves your comprehension, try reading this unusual passage: "A newspaper is better than a magazine. A seashore is a better place than a street. At first it is better to run than to walk. You may have to try several times. It takes some skill but it's easy to learn. Even young children can have fun. Once you're successful, complications are minimal. Birds seldom get too close. Too many people doing the same thing, however, can cause problems. You need lots of room. Beware of rain; it ruins everything. If there are no complications, it can be very peaceful. A rock will serve as an anchor. If things break loose from it, you will not get a second chance."

What do you think this text is about? Does it seem incomprehensible? Now look at the passage again, visualizing each sentence in terms of flying a kite. You will find it becomes clear once you have a way to "see" what it is about.

Memory and manipulation

When you are thinking visually, your memory displays an image you have called up, and you can manipulate this material to create new images. For example, call to mind a picture of the American

An illuminating ride

When Albert Einstein read a theorem explaining light waves, he reportedly imagined himself riding a light wave through space, looking back at the wave *behind him from time to time. He kept this simple image in his mind while he developed his complicated theories of light, energy, and matter.*

flag. Now change the red and white stripes to green and yellow. With your visualizing skills, you can retain the visual memory of the pattern but change the color to create a new image.

Unfortunately, the visualizing capacities of your mind are limited; you cannot hold very much material in your consciousness while you manipulate it. If you are told that the church is west of the supermarket, the supermarket is north of the stadium, the stadium is west of the parking lot, and the parking lot is south of the gas station—and then you are asked where the gas station is in relation to the church, you might have trouble visualizing the layout of the neighborhood. But you will

HOW TALL?

Draw a picture or diagram that will help you to "see" the solution to this problem: Supposing that when Mary is twice the height she is now, she will be 15 inches taller than Jean. However, Jean is at present 10 inches taller than Mary. How tall are they now? The solution is on page 139.

MARRIAGE-GO-ROUND

Finding the best way to visualize material on paper can be crucial to problem solving. Consider this puzzle: Jim, Todd, David, and Peter are all married. Their wives' names, not in any particular order, are Angela, Karen, Julie, and Cathy. Karen is Todd's sister and has three children. Jim and his wife do not have any children. Jim's wife has never met Julie, who is having an affair with Todd. Angela is so outraged by this that she is thinking of telling Todd's wife about it. Todd and David are twins. Who is married to whom?

As you try to solve the problem, you will probably start by listing the names of the people. Unfortunately, this is unlikely to help. You need to find a new way to

organize the information in some systematic way. Looking at the list, you can see that, with two categories (men and women), the problem needs to be laid out in a two-dimensional way.

On a table or matrix grid, list the men along the top and the women down one side. Draw lines between them as shown below. From the information given in the text, fill in each resulting box, using a cross to indicate that no marriage is possible, and a circle to show that the couple are married. You will see, for example, that Karen, as Todd's sister, cannot be his wife. Put an X in the corresponding box. Use the other clues to fill in the grid until you have the solution (see page 140).

find it a simple matter to answer correctly if you draw a map (as you will see, the gas station is east of the church). The map allows you to "externalize" the image. Externalization is like visualization, but it is done on paper instead of in your mind.

Family pictures

Drawing pictures or producing diagrams is particularly effective when you want to analyze how a complex set of items relate to one another—an office hierarchy, for example, or relationships in a large family. A "family tree" is a visualization that presents the relationships among people far more clearly than would ever be possible in words.

Here is a problem to solve by means of visualization: John, Wayne, Steve, and Guy all own musical instruments. John has a bassoon and an oboe, Guy has an oboe and a trumpet, Steve has a clarinet and a flute, and Wayne has a trumpet and a flute. Bassoons are cheaper than oboes, and oboes are cheaper than flutes, but trumpets are more expensive than flutes. Bassoons are more expensive than clarinets. Whose instruments cost the most? To find the answer, lay out on paper the relationships between the various instruments, and correlate these to the owners (solution on page 140).

Visual thinking, whether externalized or in your head, is often a useful approach to problem solving. It is a skill well worth acquiring.

TEST YOUR VISUALIZATION SKILLS

By using different kinds of visualization skills, you will be able to solve the four tests presented below. The solutions are on pages 140 and 141.

1. Hole in the honeycomb

This test requires you to mentally rotate objects in space. Using visualization, identify the piece (A, B, C, or D) that would exactly fit the hole in the honeycomb.

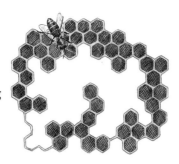

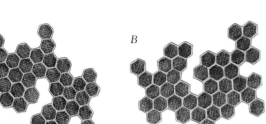

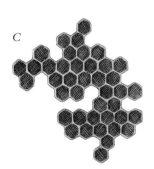

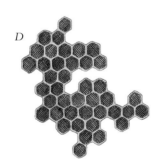

3. How many slices?

This melon has been divided with four straight cuts. All of the cuts go right through the melon. Use visualization to determine how many separate pieces of melon will result.

4. Malformations

The figure at right has been distorted, though its proportions and intersections remain the same. Can you recognize the figure as shape A, B, C, or D below?

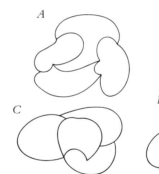

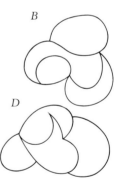

2. Twisted whale

The puzzle at right consists of 15 movable squares and one empty square. The squares can be slid up, down, or sideways into whichever space is empty. With seven moves, mentally reposition the squares so they end up forming the picture of the whale at the far right.

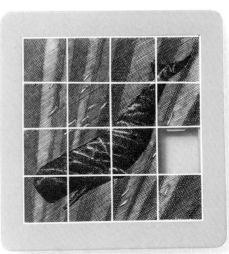

CHAPTER THREE

THE CREATIVE PROCESS

FEW HUMAN EXPERIENCES can be as rewarding as following through a sustained creative project. People who become thoroughly engaged in any area of creative activity will have found a lifelong source of satisfaction.

The process of creation begins with the learning of basic skills, the fundamental craft without which any form of self-expression is impossible. You also have to learn to seek out inspiration, keeping your eyes open for any stimulus to new ideas. After skill and inspiration comes perseverance, the staying power that will enable you to carry through a project of any scale.

It is not the purpose of this book to give instruction in any specific area of creative activity. But much of the information contained in this chapter addresses practical considerations such as the importance of providing yourself with the right equipment, the value of patterning your efforts on those of leaders in your chosen field, and simple techniques for coping with criticism.

Obstacles such as writer's block are common frustrations for the creator. A block is like a paralyzing shroud of broken confidence, a fear of failure that imprisons the victim like a straitjacket. Happily, there are several ways of breaking out of this constrictive, unproductive state. One section in this chapter gives practical tips for getting over these blocks, and suggests useful tricks for coping with interruptions.

But the creative process always involves a measure of sweat and tears. Writers, for example, often complain that every day is hard; they have to force themselves to sit at their desks, squeezing words out one by one. And everything they write is reshaped many times, and frequently rejected, before it ends up in print.

Reading about the daily frustrations faced by professionals in various creative lines of work will help you dispel any illusions about instant, smooth, or trouble-free creation. But the flip side of this cautionary note is this: Since every successful creative work is the result of application and persistence, creativity is accessible to anyone who is willing to put in the effort.

HOWEVER LARGE YOUR AMBITIONS,

EVERY CREATIVE PROJECT MUST BE APPROACHED

ONE SMALL STEP AT A TIME.

SETTING THE SCENE

How you set about launching a creative project will depend on the activity you have chosen. The process of writing pop songs, for example, does not follow the same pattern as that for inventing a board game. But to get any creative project off the ground, you need two essential elements—inspiration and craft. Everyone is familiar with the phenomenon of inspiration—the sudden flash of illumination that provides the germ of an idea for a new work or the solution to a complex problem. But if you intend to make the creative process an ongoing part of your life—whether you will be writing short stories, producing videos, or designing embroidery patterns—you will need to do more than wait passively for inspiration to come. You will have to actively pursue it.

In one sense, inspiration can be described as simply identifying a possibility. All you have to do is take a closer look at the world around you. A visit to a nearby fairground, for example, can spark a host of inventive ideas. You might start by imagining how various elements of the fairground could inspire different types of creative people. A merry-go-round might strike a novelist as a metaphor for the circular nature of time. A composer, on the other hand, might well be inspired by the carousel's

Develop an eye for detail

Inspiration can be found in most everyday situations. Cultivate the ability to pick out details from familiar scenes and exploit them for use in your own projects.

TAKE A NEW DIRECTION

Many people can master an entirely new discipline, even quite late in life. Here are ten tips for getting started in an area of creative endeavor that you have never attempted before.

1. Think carefully about the activity you are choosing. Don't embark on something unless you feel that your interest will last beyond the first flush of enthusiasm. Don't worry if your results are less than perfect in the early going.

2. Decide on your level of commitment and the limits of your ambition. Is your chosen subject going to become the focus of your life? Do you want to reach the highest level of achievement? Or are you really looking for a satisfying, but occasional, pastime?

3. Investigate the amount of equipment and materials you will need. Some activities are quite expensive to pursue properly, so it is important to determine what is appropriate to your level of commitment before you begin spending money.

4. Join a club or sign on for classes to help yourself learn the basics. If there is no appropriate facility, buy a self-instruction book.

5. Subscribe to a magazine on the subject. Almost all areas of activity have such publications, and they are often full of relevant information and practical advice.

6. Set aside designated times to concentrate on your new interest. Depending on your level of commitment, decide how much time you are willing to commit, and stick to your decision.

7. Make sure you have a suitable place to work. Some activities require peace and quiet; others take up a considerable amount of room.

8. Go out of your way in search of inspiration through observation, reading, daydreaming, or exposing yourself to new experiences.

9. Set limited goals. Decide what you want to achieve in, say, three- and six-months' time. This will motivate your efforts.

10. Show your work to others who share your interests, then discuss it with them to get their views and help clarify your own thoughts.

distinctive sounds and melodies, or a fashion designer by its brilliant whirl of colors. Similarly, a furniture maker or a sculptor might find something they could emulate in the exquisite carving of the wooden horses.

Creative people continually seek out inspiration by actively challenging their environment. Photographers are constantly asking themselves, "Would this make a good photograph?" A writer is always thinking, "Would this situation make a good story?" Some ideas will still come to you out of the blue, but you will be more open and prone to inspiration if you focus your attention on the endless possibilities around you.

Choosing a theme

The same principle applies to creativity in everyday matters. Suppose you decide to throw a party and you want to think of a theme for the event. Being observant about your surroundings can provide the inspiration you need. Perhaps as you are driving, you spy a billboard promoting tourism in Hawaii. This sets you thinking of a tropical theme for your party, complete with pineapple cocktails, tropical dishes, and Hawaiian music. You can decorate your home with exotic flowers, greet your guests with leis, and suggest they turn up in grass skirts and colorful shirts.

To develop a creative eye, it helps to have memories of a wide assortment of artistic impressions. Read a broad range of books, go to all kinds of movies, visit a variety of art galleries and museums, and travel as widely as possible. Try to take a notebook with you at all times, and instantly jot down any ideas or observations that you feel have potential for your creative projects.

The tools of the trade

Not only must you search for inspiration, you also have to develop the technical skills that will enable you to bring an idea to fruition. If you are a painter, this means knowing how to prepare a canvas and use different brushstrokes and color mixes. For a musician, it involves mastering an instrument and learning the traditional sequences of chords. If you want to try your hand at writing fiction, you will need to understand certain dramatic and narrative conventions, the ways in which a story can

MAKE A START WITH ART

To develop your visual creativity, apply a method employed by French painter and sculptor Henri Matisse. The great artist would scatter bits of colored paper onto a white sheet of paper to create a random pattern. After careful study, he would alter the patterns slightly, discovering hidden images—perhaps a snail or an exotic leaf. Finally, he would glue the scraps of paper in place.

"Frottage" is another easy-to-apply technique that can enhance creativity. German artist Max Ernst used it to produce his surreal images. He would place sheets of paper on his studio floor, then rub over them with pencil. In the patterns that emerged from the wood grain, Ernst saw shapes that reminded him of landscapes or clouds, which he would use as backgrounds for his paintings. He also developed fantasy images from the patterns.

Try creating your own fantasy pictures with torn paper, or experiment with frottage, using wood, stone, or concrete as rubbing surfaces.

Fantastic frottage
The grain in a simple plywood block provided the background effect in this artwork, depicting gentle ripples of water. Green pads of water lilies were added to make a soothing waterside scene that conveys an illusion of movement.

Striking blooms
Create colorful flowers from a rough collection of paper snippets, shaped and stuck down on paper.

unfold, and master the art of creating believable characters. A sculptor has to understand the raw materials—the grain of a block of marble, for example, or the cooling properties of metal.

Familiarity with the tools of the trade is another factor to consider, whether you are editing home videos or creating illustrations with a drawing program on your computer. No amount of innate creative ability can substitute for knowledge and technical skill; both must be acquired through study and practice. You can pick up what you need to know by reading books and magazines about your subject or by taking classes. If you are lucky, you might have the opportunity to refine your particular craft further by working with an expert. But no matter how you develop the skills, the process requires patience and perseverance.

Inspired role models

One time-honored method of learning a craft—and a good source of inspiration—is to find role models and imitate them. This need not mean that you lack originality: Imitation is a device for learning and a jumping-off point for creativity. Like most pop groups, for example, the Beatles started out by imitating rock-and-roll performers such as Chuck Berry and Buddy Holly. Their independent musical style developed later.

If you want to draw or paint, you might begin by trying to reproduce an illustration that has caught your eye in a magazine or exhibition. If you like photography, you might imitate the grainy starkness of Don McCullen's photographs or the unusual and original portrait style of Diane Arbus. Whether you are an aspiring Beverly Sills or simply a Sunday soprano, the more you study your craft, the better you will become.

Ambitious projects will almost certainly founder if you do not have the technical skills necessary for their execution. This is not a quick process. Even great artists who strive for years to master particular techniques and effects rarely, if ever, feel they have learned all they could about their craft. Think of the customer who gasps admiringly to the cabinetmaker, "You mean this took only a week to make?" "No sir," replies the craftsman, "it took 42 years and one week." The artisan reckoned that he had spent a lifetime acquiring his expertise.

USE YOUR TIME FULLY

People often feel they do not have enough time to be creative. Almost everyone, however, could make better use of his or her available time by learning how to exploit it more fully.

Here are four tips for making every waking moment work for you:

• Identify and explore any periods of "passive" time in your life—perhaps the boring stretches of time you spend traveling to work on the bus or train, eating lunch at your desk at work, sitting in a dentist's or a doctor's waiting room, or even standing in line at the supermarket checkout. No matter how busy your schedule, there are bound to be underused hours that could be taken advantage of to tap into creative thought.

In an article entitled "How I Wrote a Novel on Trains and Beside the Kitchen Sink," writer Sinclair Lewis described how, while he still had a full-time job, he constructed a novel entirely in snippets, working over breakfast before he left home in the morning and on the train while his fellow commuters were buried in their newspapers. The success of the resulting book made it possible for him to give up office work and become a professional writer.

• Familiarize yourself with the peaks and troughs of your energy levels and powers of concentration during the day; everyone is more alert at some times than at others. Then work out which periods are best suited for particular purposes—when you are better at looking for inspiration or generating new ideas, for example, or when you find it easiest to carry out complex or detailed tasks accurately.

• Establish specific routines for study and self-improvement. If you devote even half an hour of your time on a daily basis to learning about a hobby or practicing a craft, you will eventually acquire the knowledge and technical skill that constitute the foundation of all real creativity.

• Don't underestimate the creative potential of daydreaming. A long soak in the bathtub, a peaceful bask on a sunny beach, or a drowsy quarter of an hour in bed before you fall asleep could be ideal times to let your mind wander freely over problems, ideas, and possible sources of inspiration for your chosen activity or project.

PERSEVERANCE PAYS

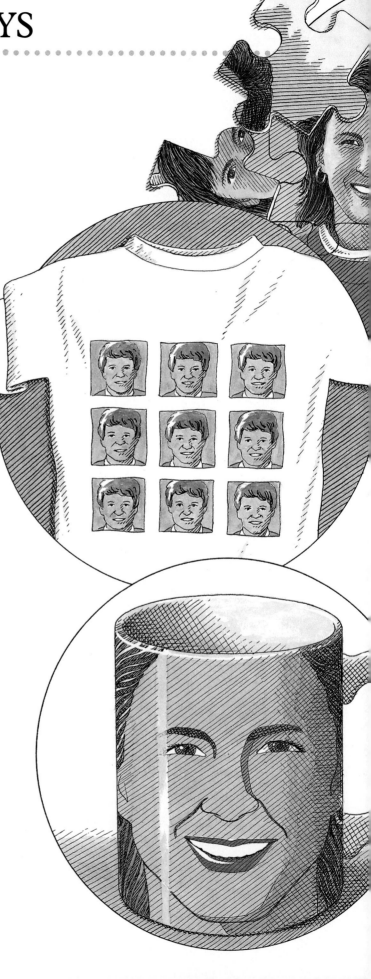

TAKING A CREATIVE IDEA through from start to finish is hard work. Between that first euphoric instant of inspiration and the satisfying moment when you see your creation completed lies a minefield of frustrations, dashed hopes, lost enthusiasm, and eroding self-esteem. To cross this divide you need more than just good ideas and optimism. You need the stamina to return to your work again and again, and a strong belief in yourself to see the project through to the end. Setbacks and interruptions are, after all, inevitable.

One of the most important steps you can take to make sure you complete a task is to be properly prepared at the start. Planning is vital. There is nothing worse than getting halfway through a project—a movie script, for example, or a painting—and then realizing that it will not work. Of course, it is in the nature of creativity that you cannot predict exactly what you are going to produce. But you need a well-conceived framework to carry you through a substantial project. It is rather like setting off to travel around the world: You won't know ahead of time what you are going to do on each day of the trip, but you will have an overall idea of the route you will take.

Sketch an outline

Here is a practical example of this type of planning: Before beginning to paint, an artist works out the composition of the picture—considering such elements as the balance of light and dark, the ratio of figures to landscape, and the overall size of the finished piece. All these points and more must be thought out to before any brushwork takes place.

Similarly, writing a book, a short story, or an article requires a plan. Most compositions have a beginning, a middle, and an end; stories need plots; characters need personalities and family histories. A structure should be worked out in advance, even if it is not strictly adhered to.

In many cases, preparation will involve not only mental planning, but also the accumulation of materials and equipment. And you will need plenty of research material as a source of ideas. The more potential input you have at your fingertips, the greater your chance of remaining stimulated and

Your best shot

With inventiveness and hard work you can develop many different creations from a single source. A simple snapshot, for example, can become a number of gifts: Transfer it onto a mug or a T-shirt, make it into a puzzle, construct it to pop out of a greeting card, inlay it on a tabletop, or perhaps turn it into unusual earrings that feature the family pet.

CREATIVE PLACES

Most people need what English novelist Virginia Woolf once described as "a room of one's own." What she had in mind was a private place where you can shut yourself away and concentrate on your creative efforts. Just putting yourself in such a place may go a long way toward helping you focus on the task at hand. The following points are well worth considering when planning such a workspace:

1. It is more difficult to work in cramped spaces. You will find it distracting and a waste of time to be continually digging out and putting away your work.

2. It helps to have the correct furnishings. A budding fashion designer, for example, will need a large table for cutting cloth, a sewing machine, an ironing board, a tailor's dummy, wardrobe-sized storage space, and drawers for patterns, sketches, threads, and tools. Jot down a list of the furniture you will need for your work.

3. The temperature of your space is all important—there is nothing more distracting than feeling too cold or too hot. Aim for a comfortable room temperature, otherwise your thinking may suffer.

4. Make sure that you have adequate light. For activities such as painting, designing clothes, or sculpting, you will need plenty of natural daylight because electric light tends to distort colors and throw unnatural shadows.

TRY AND TRY AGAIN

If you think other people find the creative process easy, read this account by Adrian Green, a journalist struggling to break into TV comedy scriptwriting:

"I have a situation and characters, but I need good plots. I scribble pages of ideas, then reject most of them because they aren't funny or fresh enough. I repeat this day after day, generating about 20 ideas a day and probably rejecting 18.

"After five days I might have three plots. I select one, then map out each scene. All this takes another few days, and only then am I ready to start writing.

"The first draft takes up to eight days of hard work. At the end, I have a 60-page script—and I spend three or four days tearing it to pieces. The second draft takes another six days, but at last it's ready to submit to a producer. His script editor points out a dozen things he

doesn't like. By now I'm fed up with the plot and tired of reworking the same gags. But I have to do it.

"The third draft is sent in. The producer likes it but his boss says 'No.' So it's back to square one."

carrying the project to completion. This period of planning and preparation serves another purpose as well: It builds up tension in the creator—a head of steam that will see you through the rough patches ahead. The creative process can be likened to running the marathon: You will need reserves of energy and stamina to finish the course. There will be times when you may want to give it all up. The creative process is rarely, if ever, a short sprint.

The right pace
Like a marathon runner, you will need to pace yourself. Establishing a routine is very important—a little every day is better than sporadic bursts of activity. Following this strategy, you will have better continuity of thought and concentration since the project will never be far from your mind.

Neil Simon, the highly successful dramatist and writer of musicals, once described his daily routine as producing three pages before noon, followed by a little tennis and some lunch, and then another few pages in the afternoon. "If I stick to a schedule like that," said Simon, "in 10 weeks I have a screenplay." Never underestimate the amount of

work you will be able to achieve in even a few hours each day. If you learned a chord sequence a week on the guitar, you would soon have a workable basis for improvisation.

To motivate yourself, it helps to set short-term goals. This allows you to experience the rewards of measurable progress. The key is to break your project down into achievable stages. But be realistic. Don't set yourself an impossible target, such as composing all the music for an album in a month when you are currently writing only a few bars a day. You may find it helpful to write out a schedule of what you hope to achieve. And take the advice given to long-distance runners: Don't look at the horizon; concentrate instead on an object about 50 to 100 yards away. That way your interest will remain high and your sense of achievement will be continually reinforced.

Occasionally, you may have a burst of creative energy and lose all sense of time. To be totally and delightfully absorbed in a task is undoubtedly one of the high points of a creative life. But it would be rare indeed to enjoy a high that carried your project from inception to completion. Routine and rhythm are more likely to see you through.

CREATIVITY IN ACTION

Any creation requires careful revision and amendment before it reaches fruition. For young London dress designer Stuart Forrester, designing a collection begins long before he makes the first cut in the fabric. He starts with a theme his clothes will portray. For the design shown here, his inspirations were recent "road" movies such as Ridley Scott's *Thelma and Louise*, and Wim Wenders' *Paris, Texas*. As Forrester comments, "By wearing one of my dresses people are in a sense taking part in their very own movie."

1. After many weeks of seeking the perfect image, dress designer Stuart Forrester came across these photos in a magazine that would provide the basic motif for his "cinema" dress.

2. The designer pasted selected images into a book in which he had highlighted relevant sentences. Viewed as a whole, they told the story of a girl traveling through the midwestern states. Then the process of design began.

3. One idea of attaching the finished image to a corset was soon rejected as "too contrived." Out, too, went the idea of a one-piece wraparound, which would have displayed little of the image. At last Forrester settled on a long A-line dress.

Grand finale
The design and making of this party dress took three months of concentrated labor. After many changes and alterations the shift finally took its place on the runway.

4. *After the final sketch was completed, a rough version of the dress was assembled using scraps of material and a dressmaker's dummy. Forrester then relied on modern technology to produce color photocopies of the final image in tiny segments on transfer paper. These were pressed on to pieces of natural cotton. The fabric sections were then carefully hand stitched together so that the image would appear seamless. Any visible stitching was painted to match the colors around it, so that the final image looked much like a movie still.*

OVERCOMING BLOCKS

WHETHER YOU PURSUE a creative activity as a casual amateur or a full-fledged professional, you will have days, or even weeks, when you feel as if your ability to generate ideas has utterly deserted you. At such times, you may feel unable to concentrate or work, and this may throw you into a state of despondency. The despondency can, in turn, quickly erode your confidence. Fortunately, there are several practical steps you can take to get the creative juices flowing again.

Essential research
Creative blocks sometimes occur when people fail to do enough research and leave themselves short of information. For example, you will get stuck writing your great novel of the Civil War if you do not know enough about that period of history. If the action, dialogue, and descriptions in your story seem stale, and you find you have only the barest outline of a plot, then you are well-advised to recognize that your preparation was too thin. The solution is additional research. The added up-front work should open up new possibilities for plot twists and interesting characters.

Whatever your area of interest, research is vital. Your creative imagination has to have material with which to work. Without it, your inner resources will quickly dry up. So if you feel stymied, look for stimulating input—in books, in conversations with other people, or wherever you can find it.

The opposite problem is too much complexity. You may be blocked because your work has become too complicated and you have created more problems than you can handle. Here the key is to simplify. Imagine creating a design for a new kitchen, for example. You might become bogged down because your plan is so ambitious that no matter which way you rearrange your drawings, you cannot squeeze all the labor-saving devices you want into the allotted space. The answer is to simplify your idea by returning to the basic concept, chopping away unnecessary frills, and finding more straightforward options.

Another all-too-common difficulty is what might be called the "first brushstroke" block. In this predicament the sight of white canvas or a

Obstruction ahead
In any creative endeavor, you run the risk of developing a block that obscures your vision and befuddles your thought processes. If your creativity dries up, you need to take positive action to surmount the problem and restore the flow.

HOW TO COPE WITH INTERRUPTIONS

An ambitious project is going to take time, so you need to be prepared to face up to the problems of stopping and starting. Many people find it difficult to dig back into the creative seam when they return to work on their project, be it the next day or a month later. Fortunately, three useful techniques can help you deal with this problem:

1. Never stop until you know what to do next
If you know what your next step will be before you stop, then it will be easier to resume work. Jot down a few ideas or visualize (see pages 72 to 75) what you are going to do next. Some writers even choose to stop in the middle of a sentence.

2. Look at your last creative outburst
Revising the material you produced at the last creative session will help you get back into your subject after a break. Before you start, look over what you have already done to put your mind back into the right groove.

3. Take the project with you
Whenever you are away from a project, use any spare moments you may have to reflect on your work and make plans for the next stage. Distancing yourself from a project for short periods of time can have beneficial effects in gaining a little perspective on what is important and what isn't.

RITUALS AND ROUTINES

If you find a special ritual that helps you start your work sessions, do not hesitate to use it. For example, it may be that the process of making a cup of coffee and switching on your telephone answering machine puts you in the mood to settle down and begin writing. Similarly, a quiet morning walk may be a useful prelude to your daily stint at the pottery wheel. Or it may be that you can only summon up your drawing skills by using a special pen or sitting in a favorite chair. Any simple ritual is beneficial as long as it puts you in a creative mode or helps you get your mind in gear.

If you depend on decidedly quirky habits to kick-start your creative flow, you are in the company of some of the world's great innovators. German poet and dramatist Friedrich Schiller could not settle down to work unless he had a rotting apple in his desk. The smell, he believed, aroused his creative powers. Russian novelist Ivan Turgenev could only work with his feet in a bucket of hot water. And French writer Honoré de Balzac always wore his favorite white dressing gown as he penned his novels.

blank page intimidates you to the point where you don't know how, or where, to begin. This problem may also be the result of a lack of preparation. Look back through your notes or plans and ask yourself if they are sufficiently thorough. If you are fully prepared for the task, your first "brushstroke" is more likely to be a strong and solid one. It may even feel like a great release.

Take the first step
Don't dawdle too long, however, before getting your project underway. Remember the proverb, "The longest journey begins with a single step." At some point, even if no inspiration is forthcoming, you must put pen to paper or brush to canvas and hope for the best. The act of getting started is sometimes enough to give you some creative momentum; you can always correct mistakes later.

Another obstacle to the creative process is adverse criticism. You show your two-thirds-finished work to friends or family, and they find fault with it. Such criticism can, of course,

be disheartening. Yet having someone else criticize your work can also be extremely helpful. The trick is to separate constructive from negative criticism.

To do this, ask yourself if those who comment adversely are showing a genuine desire to help by suggesting a better way forward, or if they are simply trying to undermine your work for reasons of their own. For example, if your partner dismisses your attempts at wood carving, is it because he or she resents the fact that you are spending so much time with a block of timber? Remember: Constructive criticism encourages you to reflect on your work, whereas destructive criticism causes you to reflect only on your relationship with the person who is criticizing your work.

Learning to recognize when to accept or reject criticism is not always easy. Good advice is almost always helpful—yet you must be careful not to fall into the trap of changing everything to suit a friend. Think through every point, and change only those that you know to be unsatisfactory.

Taking stock of the situation

You may find it difficult to tell whether you are facing a manageable creative block or the realization that your project itself is fatally flawed. The latter may be the case if your "clouded" thinking continues for a prolonged period. At some point, you will need to make a decision about the future of the project. Before you decide to ditch the entire enterprise, discuss your dilemma with other people knowledgeable in the field. They may have encountered and overcome similar obstacles.

Well-seasoned company

Artists and writers often congregate at particular cafes to meet others interested in the same pursuits. Try meeting friends regularly for a meal or a drink to discuss your work. Sharing ideas may also help you overcome a creative block.

BE FRIENDLY

Creative pursuits are often solitary ventures. Although this isolation can make it easier to concentrate on a project, it can also make it more difficult to pull yourself out of unproductive frames of mind. To overcome such blocks, try discussing your ideas with like-minded friends. Here are some suggestions:

• Join a club or attend some classes. Use these group settings to discuss the problems that are keeping you from accomplishing your creative goals. Just voicing your fears to others may suggest a way out of the difficulty.

• Pay regular visits to a restaurant or favored meeting place frequented by people engaged in your line of work. Or start up your own social group of like-minded individuals. Einstein did this when he created the "Olympia Society," a group of three or four friends who met weekly to share a meal and exchange ideas.

• If it is not possible to arrange such a gathering, try using the mail, the telephone, or, if possible, computer bulletin boards to communicate with others. The great naturalist Charles Darwin lived a retiring life but maintained a vast network of correspondents.

• From time to time you may need to make yourself more conspicuous and present yourself and your work to the world, risking criticism perhaps, but also inviting praise. The reaction of strangers to different aspects of what you have done may give you a new slant on how to approach the work.

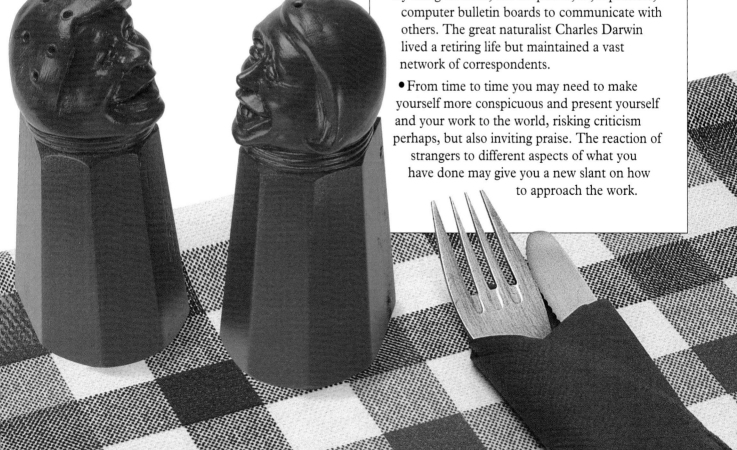

CHAPTER FOUR

GROUP CREATIVITY

NOT ALL CREATIVE ACTS are carried out in solitude. Successful innovation or problem solving is very often a group effort, the result of teamwork rather than of private endeavor. Some of the most popular creative forms of expression are the product of collective effort, among them the movies, television, theatre, music, and magazines.

Since the 1950s, a host of experts have devoted themselves to devising methods that will encourage and exploit group creativity—brainstorming is the most famous example—because innovation has become vital to the modern economy. However, many of the ideas advanced by these theorists, such as the need for an open flow of information or the importance of working in small teams, have been slow to take hold in major organizations.

The main advantage you have as a member of a team is that you can contribute in those areas where you are strongest and let others cover for your shortcomings. This chapter will show you how to determine which of eight recognized roles best suits you on a team, and how to make the most of creative role-playing in addressing a wide range of problems.

Encouraging creativity at work does not require the work force to behave like delinquents or start wearing silly clothes. It actually means happier managers, more fulfilled employees, more interesting work and, most importantly for the success of the company, larger profits.

In this chapter you will read how companies can foster creativity by giving their employees time to come up with new ideas; how laughing with others can help you crack stubborn problems; and why employees should be encouraged to risk making mistakes.

If you put some of these ideas into practice, working with other people can become a rewarding and inspiring experience. An employee who has the chance to chip away creatively at a problem with a team will feel a real sense of achievement after completing the task. Solving problems together helps a group to forge durable bonds of trust and mutual respect.

A TEAM OF INDIVIDUALS, EACH WITH DIFFERENT

ABILITIES, CAN COLLABORATE TO TAKE EVEN THE MOST

DIFFICULT PROJECT FROM IDEA TO REALITY.

IMAGINATION AT WORK

NOT SURPRISINGLY, INDIVIDUALS who develop creative skills at home also devise ways of applying those abilities at work. Yet, although an employee of an organization may find it relatively easy to come up with imaginative solutions to his or her specific job demands, the task of getting the entire organization to embrace the goal of creativity often poses more daunting challenges.

In a sense, many companies are victims of their own top-heavy organization. Under pressure to be more profitable, they often create inflexible systems and end up hamstrung by their own bureaucracy. At worst, employees in such companies become little more than robots, their personal expression suppressed in the name of productivity. Restrictive job titles, fixed hierarchies, and cumbersome communication systems can keep the best employee ideas from ever being implemented.

Survival of the fittest

Personal creativity can, however, be successfully nurtured within the corporate framework. Indeed, companies must encourage employee initiative if they wish to stay alive in today's highly competitive markets. Survival in business increasingly depends on how well companies are able to respond to changing consumer demands. A business must continually develop new products, improve services, break into fresh markets, and discover novel ways of keeping its overhead low. For many organizations, the difference between profitability and decline will lie in their ability to come up with new ideas.

Companies have often found that those employees in direct contact with customers are in the best position to detect where and how changes need to be made. The people at the top of an organization are often too far removed from the day-to-day operations and problems to recognize the need for change. Yet, companies often restrict the innovative potential of their lower-level employees by imposing rigid job descriptions, by limiting their employees' access to financial

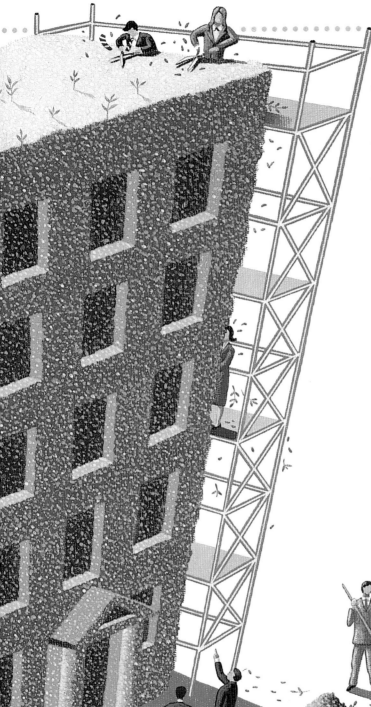

The need for nurture
Maximizing a company's potential for growth is rather like cultivating a garden. Just as plants need nurturing, so does employee creativity.

information, and by providing little opportunity for on-the-spot decision making.

One fundamental way a company can encourage creativity is by dismantling its existing power structure. In most companies, power is determined by your place in a hierarchy. The main drawback of this traditional system is that the bosses at the top usually try to maximize their power by withholding information from those at lower levels. If employees don't know where problems exist, how can they help to solve them?

Greater freedom

To prevent this stockpiling of information, some companies have dispensed with confining job titles that limit an employee's activities. A number of organizations have also found it helpful to adopt a less enclosed physical setting for their staff, opting for an open-plan design rather than individual offices. This encourages greater interaction and, as a result, may enhance creativity.

The size of a workgroup can also affect creativity. The vast multi-layered bureaucracy that develops in large companies tends to induce conformity and suppress innovation. Corporations benefit from being broken down into small divisions in which everyone can get to know one another and exchange ideas.

Restructuring the corporate power structure was one of the major changes implemented by Sarah Nolan at the California-based Amex Life Assurance Company, when she became president in 1986. The company had been performing sluggishly for several years. Nolan recognized that part of Amex Life's problem was its rigid hierarchy, which offered few opportunities for creative exchanges among workers doing different jobs. Nolan asked her managers to set up an entirely different style of office, one that was much more open. A computer was placed on each desk, giving employees access to all available information about the company, including data previously held only by top management. Job distinctions were purposely blurred, and management began to encourage innovation. Employees at all levels consequently felt an increased sense of responsibility and involvement. As a result, the company became much more responsive to customer needs—and its profits increased dramatically.

Equal responsibilities

Skaltek, a highly successful heavy machinery producer in Stockholm, Sweden, has fostered employee creativity from its inception. When its founder, Öystein Skalleberg, set up the company after leaving a conventionally organized firm, he was determined not to emulate what he calls "the defend my box in the hierarchy" mentality.

As a consequence, no one at Skaltek has a privileged status, and everyone has the same job title. At weekly meetings, all employees receive a full report of the previous week's cash flow. Everyone knows the financial position of the company, and salaries are subject to open discussion. All machines produced at the company bear the signatures of key workers. This enables employees to register their pride in what they produce. Skalleberg maintains that if people feel a sense of responsibility for their work, they will be more inclined to look for imaginative solutions to any problems that arise.

Action required

Many senior executives, who agree in principle that creativity is a valuable asset, balk at actually introducing methods to promote it, claiming that pressing everyday needs must take priority.

For this reason, Edward de Bono, the creativity expert who coined the term "lateral thinking" (see page 50), believes that it is virtually essential for a company to appoint a "creative process champion." This should be a senior executive with explicit responsibility for developing creative skills among the personnel. The executive who takes on such a job must first help his fellow managers understand

INNOVATING FOR PROFIT

In 1974, Arthur Fry was singing in the choir of his church in Minnesota. To his annoyance, the scraps of paper marking the places in his hymnal kept falling out. He decided he needed bookmarks that would self-attach without damaging the book. In a flash of inspiration, Fry, a chemical engineer, remembered a low-tack adhesive invented by a colleague. It had been abandoned as a failure—who needed a glue that didn't stick permanently?

The company that Fry worked for, Minnesota Mining & Manufacturing (3M), has various policies designed to encourage creativity. One, known as "bootlegging," allows scientists to spend 15 percent of their work time on projects of their own choosing. Fry decided to use his bootleg time to develop sticky bookmarks. In the course of his research, he also realized that people could write notes on his easily attachable and detachable stickers. This brainstorm marked the birth of the original Post-it Notes, now one of the top five office products sold in the United States. This story amply demonstrates how a company's positive encouragement of creativity can lead to a commercial success.

In order to bring about a valuable exchange of information and ideas throughout the company, 3M created a technology council where researchers from

Versatile stationery
Post-its, launched in 1980, transformed office life. They are now sold around the world.

various divisions meet regularly. This procedure has resulted in such imaginative products as the Scotch-Brite scourer-sponge, created by nonwoven-fiber experts and abrasives scientists working together.

Another 3M mandate requires that at least 25 percent of a division's sales should result from products introduced within the previous five years. As a result of this policy, 3M researchers are constantly coming up with new ideas, and the company has created more than 60,000 products. These range from its well-known adhesive tapes to heart-lung machines, anti-static videotape, synthetic ligaments for damaged knees, and heavy-duty reflective sheeting for construction-site signs.

Technological hotspot

Some innovative companies work in isolation. An area outside San Francisco, however, became a magnet for upstart innovators. Known popularly as "Silicon Valley" after the material from which semiconductor chips are made, the area has been home since the 1970s to a host of highly innovative microelectronics and computer software companies. The products of these companies not only earn phenomenal profits but have had a profound effect on popular culture. Instrumental to Silicon Valley's success has been a fertile business climate—the result of a close relationship between the Valley's expanding entrepreneurial industries and Stanford University.

Creative spirit in this region also benefits from a highly mobile workforce that socializes freely. The resulting informal contact spawns a fruitful interchange of ideas, information, and enthusiasm.

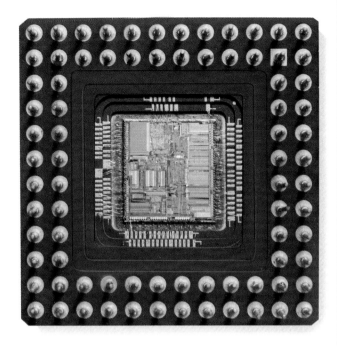

Small but profitable
Thanks to the tiny but powerful silicon chip, Silicon Valley grew into a revenue-producing powerhouse that is at the leading edge of technology.

A problem taped
One of the earliest inventions that resulted from 3M's policy of encouraging creativity was masking tape. It was invented during the 1920s by Richard G. Drew, after he observed that painters on auto-assembly lines were having difficulty keeping borders straight on two-tone cars.

exactly what creativity means and why it needs to be valued. This might involve organizing "creativity awareness" seminars to which senior executives from all parts of the company are invited. Once the people at the top levels of the company have come to accept the idea of a more creative workplace, the designated "creative process champion" can then go on to set up training seminars in which all employees are taught lateral thinking and other creative problem-solving techniques.

Suggestion schemes

One way to encourage employees to contribute innovative ideas is to set up a suggestion scheme. But it needs to be one in which employees are actively encouraged to come forth with their ideas. This is business as usual in Japan where the Toyota Motor Company, for example, receives around 300 suggestions per employee every year. By contrast, the average Western company receives fewer than 10.

One reason that Japanese suggestion schemes are so successful is that an employee's idea is considered first by his or her peers: Employees usually feel more comfortable offering ideas to their colleagues than they do submitting them to management. De Bono recommends requesting ideas from employees on specific topics over limited time periods. The topic in focus during one month might be "cost-saving," during another month it might be "safety."

Unfortunately, communication in large, hierarchical organizations tends to run only from the top down. Although this process permits commands to be issued along clear-cut channels, it also has the adverse effect of stifling creative thinking, which is stimulated by the exchange of ideas. Conversely, two-way communication, in which employees ask questions and offer opinions, encourages creativity. It may be a lengthier process and it spreads power away from the top, but it has proved to be far more valuable in the long term.

Risky pay off

Most people shy away from taking risks in the workplace because promotion, pay, and prestige are often at stake. But a certain amount of risk-taking is essential to growth—both personal and corporate. There is a big difference, however, between recklessness and prudent risk-taking. Billionaire

HOW CREATIVE IS YOUR WORKPLACE?

If you work for an organization that is truly concerned about encouraging creativity among its staff, you should find that you are able to answer "yes" to at least five of the following questions.

1. If you had an idea for a new project or procedure, could you present it to your boss without the fear of looking foolish or overstepping the mark?

2. Does management hold brainstorming sessions or otherwise encourage the contribution of new ideas?

3. Do you have free access to financial and other information about the company?

4. Is your job description fairly loose, allowing you to contribute in a variety of ways suited to your particular skills and interests?

5. Are you given the opportunity to make decisions at work based on your own judgment?

6. Do people in your company work in small teams so that they can readily exchange ideas?

7. Are any innovations suggested by employees financially rewarded—or even acknowledged?

8. Does your company provide seminars, courses, or workshops in creative thinking techniques or in creative problem solving?

9. Do you work in an open-plan office where creative suggestions can be freely exchanged?

10. Are you confident that your boss would give you credit for your ideas, rather than steal them?

businessman John Paul Getty, for example, didn't get rich by having the intemperate instincts of a riverboat gambler. He took calculated chances—a characteristic of the creative personality (see pages 28 to 33). To encourage this attitude, and to encourage willingness among its employees to challenge old ideas, the Midwest Energy Company in Sioux City, Iowa, sends its personnel on an out-door adventure/learning course called "Playing to Win." The program requires participants to col-laborate on tasks that demand both physical and emotional effort. Through learning to trust and cooperate with their col-leagues, the company's employees gain the confi-dence to take creative risks.

Setting up the right con-ditions for innovation also make for a happier work force. In their book *The Creative Spirit,* Daniel Goleman, Paul Kaufman, and Michael Ray

write: "Many workers are no longer in search of a job that is simply a source of wealth, status and power, but rather one that—apart from assuring a decent living—offers a sense of meaning and a plat-form for individual creativity." The resourceful modern employer will attempt to meet this need.

A slice of the company cake
To encourage their staff to be innovative, employers should offer prizes for ideas that prove successful. Recognition in the form of expense-paid vacations, meal vouchers, or even flower bouquets can be effective ways of expressing appreciation. Honoring achievements by publicizing them at a ceremony also makes creative employees feel more valued.

BETTER BRAINSTORMING

As A SENIOR EXECUTIVE of a large New York advertising firm during the 1950s, Alex Osborn was looking for a way to encourage his staff to generate imaginative new ideas for advertising campaigns. The technique he came up with was "brainstorming"—a group activity in which all the members of the group put forward as many ideas as possible without worrying about the immediate value or logic of their remarks. The object was to shake up people's ideas and help them break away from predictable and often unsatisfactory ways of thinking or problem solving.

Freedom of expression
Osborn established six basic rules for successful brainstorming:

1. Participants should generate the wildest ideas possible. For this reason a freewheeling, almost manic, atmosphere must be encouraged. Osborn insisted that it is easier to tame crazy ideas—tailoring them to fit the company's needs—than it is to try to make dull thinking more exciting.

2. There should be no criticism during the brainstorming session itself; evaluation should follow at a later stage. This is to prevent people in full creative flow from becoming distracted by the need to defend their suggestions.

3. The group must be encouraged to come up with as many ideas as possible. When people are not censored immediately, they tend to contribute more freely. Osborn believed that sheer quantity of ideas leads to a greater number of valuable ones.

4. Group members should try to build upon or modify contributions from others. A wild notion may not be useful as it stands, but adapting it or combining it with other ideas may produce an exciting and workable solution to a problem. As one person pursues a particular theme, others in the group should chip in with related thoughts.

5. An experienced leader should be appointed to generate the right atmosphere, to ensure that the rules are followed, and to encourage everyone to participate. The leader should not dominate the group, but simply act as an objective chairperson.

6. It is essential that someone take notes of the ideas generated, or—better still—that the entire session be tape-recorded, so that even the smallest comment can be remembered and evaluated.

Osborn promoted the technique of brainstorming through books and seminars, and it became extremely popular during the 1950s. Dozens of American companies began training personnel in the technique, and many of them later reported impressive successes in generating both new concepts and workable answers to specific problems.

Too many cooks
The popularity of brainstorming led to the notion that deliberate creative thinking must be a collective effort. Osborn even suggested that the average person "can think up twice as many ideas when working with a group." But some subsequent research has revealed that groups are not necessarily more effective at brainstorming than individuals. In a study conducted during the early 1960s, one psychologist found that individual brainstorming produced 30 to 40 percent more original and innovative suggestions than emerged from the groups, and that the quality of the suggestions was higher in practical terms. Why? The study showed that groups tend to spend too much time developing a single train of thought. Further, some individuals become inhibited in a group and feel unable to contribute. The study concluded that individual brainstorming may be the most effective method if it follows a warm-up group session.

Individual benefit
In his book *Serious Creativity*, Edward de Bono writes, "In my experience, individuals on their own produce far more ideas and a far wider range of ideas than when they are working together in a group." Yet, although he argues that individuals are better at initiating concepts, De Bono believes that groups are better at developing them.

One approach that combines the advantages of both individual and group brainstorming—and that

---

Squeezing out ideas
When thoughts are freely expressed, the results can be profitable! If each member of a brainstorming group gives uninhibited expression to any *idea he or she may have, an ingenious new concept or solution may emerge. The silliest suggestion can sometimes spark off a winner.*

avoids the dilemma of which one should come first—is the "sandwich method." Here individuals work independently, then bring their ideas to a group session. Afterward each person brainstorms some more on his or her own, then returns to the group for a final session.

Favorable conditions

Whether used in conjunction with individual brainstorming or on its own, group brainstorming has been found to work best if certain organizing principles are followed. One is to bring together the right mix of people. During the early 1970s, research by psychologist Thomas Bouchard showed that groups outshine individuals at brainstorming when the groups include individuals with expertise from a variety of disciplines.

Bouchard also discovered that groups are much more effective if each member is called upon in turn to contribute. Involving all of the group's members prevents any single person from dominating the process and inhibiting the others.

A number of psychologists have also challenged Osborn's original assertion that the success of brainstorming depends on withholding criticism until ideas have been exhausted. One research study compared the number and quality of ideas produced by groups instructed in standard brainstorming techniques and in a more critical approach. The more critical groups were instructed to try to think logically, and to produce good, practical suggestions. The wilder flights of fantasy traditionally associated with brainstorming were discouraged. The researchers found that, although the critical approach resulted in fewer ideas than did traditional brainstorming, it produced approximately the same number of high-quality ideas.

The practical approach

Many psychologists now believe that to achieve the most satisfactory results in problem-solving sessions, the group should always be presented with a list of practical criteria that any possible solution must meet.

For example, if members of a production team are asked to come up with a brand-new way of packaging a peanut, they should also be told that their solutions must meet specific guidelines—the packaging must be inexpensive, for example, air-tight, or ecologically sound. All involved will then be mindful of the boundaries within which they must work to complete the project successfully.

Business solutions

An interesting variant on the brainstorming concept is synectics, which brings together people of diverse abilities to address problems. Developed in the 1950s and 1960s by George M. Prince and William Gordon, this technique strongly encourages free-associating of nonrational ideas.

MAXIMIZING SUCCESS

It is now generally believed that a group brainstorming session needs a certain amount of structuring and discipline if it is to be really effective. If you are organizing such a session, here are some guidelines you can apply to enhance your chances of success:

• Keep the number of people in the group to six, seven, or eight.

• Allocate a fixed amount of time for the session and stick to it. The mind can work with amazing speed when faced with a deadline.

• Appoint a leader who can be positive, can control the session without dominating it, and can prevent the group from pursuing one train of thought for too long.

• Structure the session, asking each person in turn to contribute ideas.

• Remind members they must concentrate on the task at hand. It is all too easy for minds to wander during a creative thinking session.

• Set clear and precise criteria that the solution must meet.

• Try not only to generate plenty of ideas but to obtain some practical solutions to problems.

• Encourage members to build on others' ideas.

• Ideally, tape record the session. If this is impracticable, appoint one member to take notes.

Hot idea

When telephone wires in Oregon kept snapping under the weight of ice and snow, telephone company executives held a brainstorming session to find a remedy. The ideas generated at this session ran the gamut from the hopelessly impractical to the extremely helpful. One idea put forward was to bury the wires underground. Another was to wrap them in fur coats to keep them warm. One person suggested that airplanes with heating pads strapped underneath should fly low over the wires to melt the ice. Although this suggestion was impractical, it led to the notion of using helicopters for the task. This proved highly successful. The helicopters could fly low and slow over the wires, and the heat from their exhausts melted the ice and snow.

DO-IT-YOURSELF BRAINSTORMING

You can use brainstorming techniques to tackle problems in your own life. To learn how, try the following three-stage brainstorming exercise.

Imagine that you have the opportunity to purchase a second home, but you don't know what sort of property to buy. To brainstorm your way to the right decision, begin by writing the trigger label "Second home" at the top of a sheet of paper. Underneath it, itemize all the different types of residences that a second home suggests to you. Try to come up with at least eight different ideas.

Now go through the list, jotting down at least two positive aspects of each suggestion. Avoid self-censorship at this stage—wacky ideas are as valuable as sensible ones. Your responses might be as follows:
Country house—healthy, open-air life; friendly neighborhood atmosphere; keep chickens.
City apartment—suitable for entertaining business contacts; easy access to the city center.

Mountain shack—hikes in beautiful surroundings; skiing in the winter; possible friendship with bears.
Beach house—water sports; great for parties.
Farm—space for friends to stay; cheap manure.
Desert island—plenty of sun; no need to dress up.
Trailer—travel where you like; picturesque; could lend to film studios as movie prop.
Igloo—a real escape; fresh fish available; plentiful ice for cocktails; quiet.

Evaluate your list
Now examine your responses to see if they trigger any new thoughts. Your comment about the cheap manure, for example, may remind you that farm animals might not appreciate your dog. Or the note about the fish may reconfirm your preference for fresh, plain food. You may also notice that references to social activities and the beauty of the surroundings keep cropping up. So although the mountain shack and the desert island appeal in many ways, you realise that you would prefer to be somewhere more accessible to visiting friends. The beach house now seems like the best bet, with its ideal combination of fresh fish, an ever-changing view, room to entertain friends, and space outside where your dog can run freely.

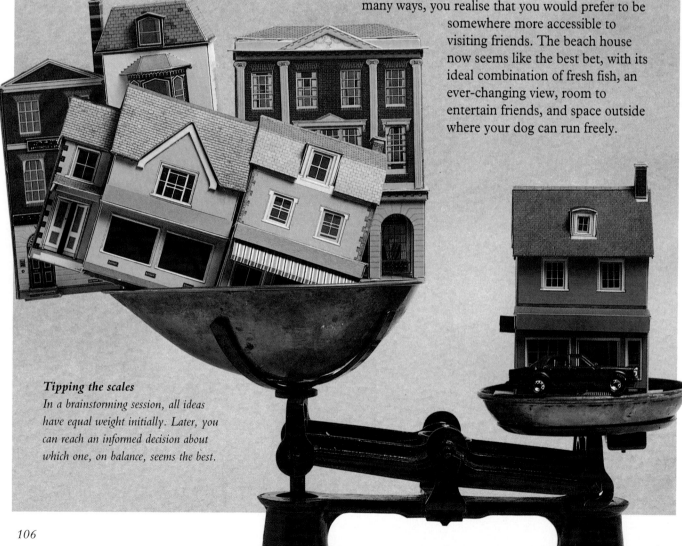

Tipping the scales
In a brainstorming session, all ideas have equal weight initially. Later, you can reach an informed decision about which one, on balance, seems the best.

Material success

A synectics group once tackled the assignment of finding a use for the crushed glass produced when old cars are compacted. One member of the group commented that the crushed glass made him think of sugar crystals. This led him to thoughts of how cotton candy is made. He suggested melting the glass, then using centrifugal force to spray it against the inner walls of a spinning cylinder, resulting in spun glass. The end product was a major new material, fiberglass, now used for heat and sound insulation, and also for the manufacture of textiles and plastics.

A typical synectics group consists of approximately six people, each from a different background or profession. During a session, which lasts about 45 minutes, the problem is first analyzed so that it is fully understood, then possible solutions are suggested. As in brainstorming, participants are encouraged to suggest things they would normally dismiss as ridiculous. In order to generate unusual ideas, members of the group are asked to employ four different mechanisms: personal analogy, direct analogy, symbolic analogy, and fantasy analogy.

Identify with the problem

Personal analogy provokes new ideas by asking each person to identify with the problem at hand. If, for example, the group is trying to invent a new kind of clothing fastener, members might imagine being the fastener, then try to describe how its mechanism works.

Direct analogy helps spark ideas by asking each group member to compare the key element in the problem with something very similar in structure or function. A camera, for example, might be compared to an eye. Symbolic analogy, on the other hand, works by having the members link the problem to an object they believe symbolizes it. A protective material, for example, might be identified with a guard dog.

The final mechanism for generating ideas in a synectics group is fantasy analogy. Here, each person is asked to invoke a fantastic concept about the problem at hand, such as imagining a computer that is able to read the user's thoughts.

Looking for these analogies stimulates the unconscious mind to bring forth ideas that would not otherwise surface. In addition, it discourages early judgment and helps to structure the session by forcing participants to examine ideas from a variety of intriguing angles.

Freedom to invent

Synectics is more structured and complex than brainstorming, which emphasizes quantity rather than quality. But the two approaches share the same philosophy: Creative solutions present themselves only through a free exchange of ideas.

Clearly, not every session of synectics or brainstorming will be productive. The key to success lies as much in the interpretation of the suggestions as in the quality or quantity of the ideas themselves. It is vital to keep a relaxed, playful atmosphere in the group—joking around gives participants the freedom to express zany ideas. Research has shown that a team whose members are ready to laugh is often more creative than an overly serious group.

INSPIRED TEAMWORK

MOST LARGE ORGANIZATIONS now recognize that their size can be a handicap to creativity. As a result, many have begun developing small working teams to encourage innovation from their employees. Individuals who work together in small groups tend to feel a greater sense of personal responsibility for solving problems and completing the task at hand. It is not enough, however, simply

George M. Prince, who devised the synectics theory of problem solving (see pages 104 and 107), believes that the importance of group dynamics should not be overlooked. Certain attitudes and actions, he stresses, need to be actively encouraged within the group to help promote cooperation and creativity. To begin with, Prince says, the individuals participating in the group should all have diverse

to throw together a group of individuals and expect them to be creative at the drop of a hat. It is essential to choose people who can work well together and to train them in creative-thinking techniques. Each team also needs a strong leader, someone who can bring out the best in each member of the group and yet keep the team focused on its predetermined goal.

The right approach

A secure and accepting environment is vital for the group to succeed. Otherwise, working in a small team can cause some individuals to feel exposed and insecure about making mistakes.

Creative thinking requires people to take risks, sometimes at the expense of appearing foolish in front of colleagues. A team member's reluctance to take such risks can jeopardize the whole creative process. But if the right atmosphere of security and acceptance is created, then everyone feels empowered to participate fully and without restraint.

personalities. Moreover, they must treat each other as equals—status and rank should be eliminated for the length of the project. One particularly interesting feature of the synectics process is that the leader does not contribute directly to solving the problem, but simply records what is said and ensures the smooth running of the session. By keeping the leader out of the problem-solving process, you encourage the group to remain noncompetitive.

Prince also stresses that a positive attitude must be maintained throughout the group session. To this end, he urges adherence to the following rules: Every member of the group has to assume that a solution to the problem at hand is attainable. If a group member wants to air a negative comment, he or she can only make it after voicing two positive statements. Each member of the group must also take individual responsibility for his or her participation. In addition, members must pledge not to be pessimistic, bored, or distracted. They must avoid the temptation to compete or to try to dominate

Working in harmony
Small teams, in which people draw on one another's strengths, promote creativity. A jazz band is a perfect example of this principle. Although each musician has the opportunity to take the lead from time to time, and to give expression to his or her skills, the individualism is subordinate to teamwork.

ON THE BALL

In the 1880s, James Naismith, a physical education coach at Springfield College in Massachusetts, became aware of the need for a winter game that could be played indoors. The only existing form of indoor exercise at the time was rhythmic bodily exercises, which most students found boring.

Naismith and his students began a creative experiment in the gym. Working as a group, they set out to develop a new ball game for two competing teams that would be safe to play on a hard surface and in a limited space.

Gradually, Naismith and his students established rules for their new game. They decided that bats, sticks, or rackets were out because they made sport too tough and dangerous. They banned running while carrying the ball and physical contact between players. After two weeks of trial and error, a new sport took shape that conformed to these limits.

A fortnight of creative teamwork had produced what has since become one of the most popular games in the world—basketball.

others. Nor should they interrupt or criticize other members of the group.

In addition to removing social inhibitions among the group members, it may be necessary to jog them out of their usual, well-worn thought tracks. Techniques such as lateral thinking (see pages 50 to 55) and brainstorming (pages 102 to 107) provide effective methods of doing this.

An alternative approach to group problem solving is sociodrama, which is another variation on brainstorming. Members of a sociodrama group first define the problem, then address it within a dramatic form. Each individual assumes a role in the drama, which is then acted out through improvisation. For example, if the problem is to find a new way of packaging and advertising a skincare product, one group member might play the part of the product, proclaiming its benefits ("I make your skin feel even smoother..."), while others might take on the roles of salesman ("The revolutionary discovery of collagen helps your skin to..."), satisfied customer ("I feel and look younger..."), dissatisfied customer ("It is expensive..."), and so on. Dramatic dialogues are encouraged, and a player can question any other.

The sociodrama director can change the course of the play or stop it at any point. At the end, the group discusses any noteworthy ideas that may have emerged from the playacting.

Dramatic effects

Advocates of sociodrama believe that it enables people to tap into a deeper layer of problem-solving abilities than is normally accessible. Educational psychologist E. Paul Torrance, who popularized the technique during the 1970s, asserts that "playing a role permits a person to go beyond himself and shed some of the inhibitions that stifle the production of alternative solutions. Playing a role gives a person a kind of license to think, say, and do things he would not otherwise do."

Another way to foster creativity within groups is to keep problem-solving teams flexible. Brainstorming and synectics groups are often ad hoc gatherings—set up exclusively to solve a particular problem. They have a single directive to follow and a short lifespan, two factors that tend to instill a sense of urgency among participants. Group stagnation can also be avoided by rotating people through different teams. This keeps the participants interested in the process of team problem solving while encouraging them to view obstacles and solutions from as many different perspectives as possible.

The effectiveness of a team depends on the qualities of its individual members. Robert Sternberg, a psychologist from Yale university who has studied the measurement of IQ, believes that groups of people may have collective IQs. He also suggests that the combined intellectual abilities of a group working well together can surpass the sum of the individual intelligences in the group.

The makeup of any problem-solving group needs to be carefully considered. If a team has been set up to produce solutions to a specific problem, the inclusion of outsiders—people who are unfamiliar with the problem—can be very valuable.

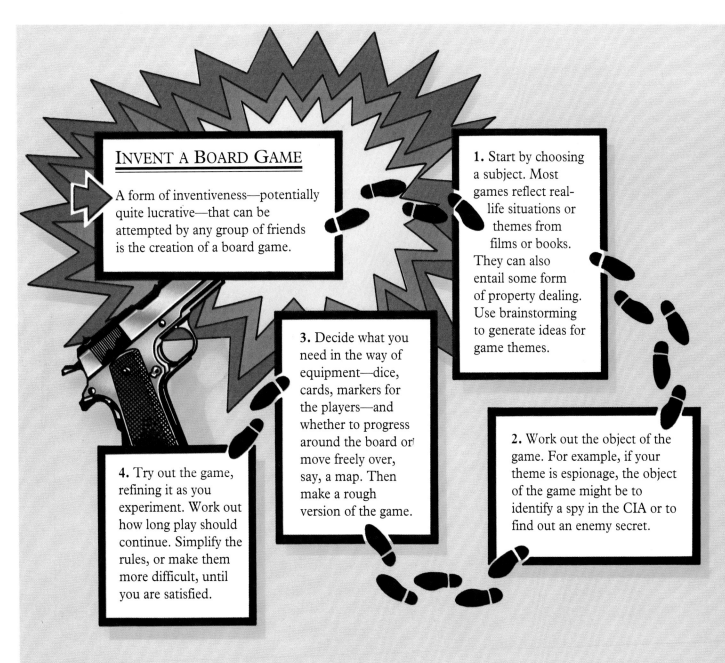

INVENT A BOARD GAME

A form of inventiveness—potentially quite lucrative—that can be attempted by any group of friends is the creation of a board game.

1. Start by choosing a subject. Most games reflect real-life situations or themes from films or books. They can also entail some form of property dealing. Use brainstorming to generate ideas for game themes.

2. Work out the object of the game. For example, if your theme is espionage, the object of the game might be to identify a spy in the CIA or to find out an enemy secret.

3. Decide what you need in the way of equipment—dice, cards, markers for the players—and whether to progress around the board or move freely over, say, a map. Then make a rough version of the game.

4. Try out the game, refining it as you experiment. Work out how long play should continue. Simplify the rules, or make them more difficult, until you are satisfied.

Of course, the personalities of those who make up the team are a critical factor in whether or not it will succeed. Psychologist R. Meredith Belbin at the Industrial Training Research Unit in Cambridge, England, carried out extensive research in the 1970s to find out what makes a successful team. He discovered that teams consisting of similar personalities tended to perform more poorly than teams with a variety of temperaments and talents. But, when the right combination of people comes together, complementary talents can make the creative process seem almost effortless.

Natural roles
Belbin analyzed the parts that different personalities tend to play in teams. He eventually identified eight distinct roles (see "Discover your team role" on pages 114 to 115). The most successful teams, of course, are those that include members who are suited to each of these different roles and whose strengths do not overlap.

The ideal number of people on a team seems to be six to eight people. Larger teams tend to make it more difficult for everyone to have a say. Smaller teams, on the other hand, often require that each member play several different roles, including one or two that may be unsuitable.

On the whole, well-planned and well-led groups offer expertise, motivation, and emotional support to the participants. Teams can also accomplish tasks that individuals cannot. For this to happen, however, they must be prepared to learn and put into practice the many factors that are favorable to creativity.

THINKING HATS

Effective thought requires a flexible outlook. Edward de Bono has described six different modes of thinking, ranging from intuitive to more objective approaches. He associated each different mode of thinking with a particular color in "thinking hats"—white, red, black, yellow, green, and blue.

White hat White is a neutral color, and this hat symbolizes objective thought. A typical approach is "What are the facts of the matter?"

Red hat Red represents fire and warmth, as well as emotional, intuitive thinking. A red-hat thinker is led mainly by his or her gut feelings.

Black hat Black is the color of negativity and severity. The black hat is worn for criticizing or objecting. A person wearing a black hat might argue "We don't have the staff to do that."

Yellow hat Yellow is the color of sunlight; this hat represents optimism and positive thought. A yellow-hat thinker may try to make things happen by coming out

GROUP CREATIVITY / INSPIRED TEAMWORK

with statements such as "People would pay more for the higher quality."

Green hat Green stands for fertility and growth. Thus, the green hat represents ideas that are either new or the offshoots of others. To break obvious thinking patterns, a green-hat thinker may say "How about trying a totally different way?"

Blue hat Blue is the color of the sky. It symbolizes the overview. The blue-hat thinker compares different opinions and sums up the group's views and findings.

De Bono suggested that a problem-solving group can be more effective if its members deliberately adopt several or all of the six modes. This can be done in a variety of ways. Each member can "wear" a different hat and advance the views appropriate to that hat; or half the team can wear a yellow hat, the other half a green hat; or the entire group can wear a hat of the same color, then switch to another. Whatever the method used, the intention is the same—to make people adopt new ways of thinking, and in the process open up new channels of creativity.

The six hats can also help individual creative thinking. If you are struggling with a recurring problem, it may be that your thinking is too rigid. Try wearing each of De Bono's hats in turn to force yourself to take a variety of approaches; you may discover a wholly original solution.

Which hat do you wear?
Most people incline toward certain types of thinking. To find out which ones you favor, write down the colors of the six hats, with the numbers 0 to 9 beside each one. Then consider the definitions at left and score yourself on a rating from 0 to 9, underlining the range of numbers that represents the degree to which you normally wear each hat.

If, for example, you see yourself as often being rather critical in your thinking (a rating of, say, 5), but know that in certain situations you adopt a hypercritical approach (8 or 9), then draw a line next to **Black**, beneath the numbers 5 to 9. If you feel you are rarely optimistic about the outcome of any problem, then underline 0 and 1 next to **Yellow**.

Sample chart
The following chart shows how you might fill in your scores.

White	0	1	2	3	4	5	6	7	8	9
Red	0	1	2	3	4	5	6	7	8	9
Black	0	1	2	3	4	5	6	7	8	9
Yellow	0	1	2	3	4	5	6	7	8	9
Green	0	1	2	3	4	5	6	7	8	9
Blue	0	1	2	3	4	5	6	7	8	9

This is a fairly objective thinker, rarely allowing emotion to overrule judgment; he or she is more positive than negative. Although rather short on original ideas, this person is able to draw the threads of an argument together to arrive at a conclusion.

Interpreting your own chart
Underlining a wide range of numbers next to a particular color shows that you are flexible in your use of that type of thinking. A small range indicates that you think this way to a consistent degree. A small-range high score suggests that you may be too set in that way of thinking. A small-range low score means that you consistently underutilize that style of thinking and might benefit from using it more.

DISCOVER YOUR TEAM ROLE

This test, developed by psychologist R. Meredith Belbin, reveals which role you tend to assume on a team. Read through each of the sections **1** through **6**, and distribute 10 points among the sentences **a** to **h**, according to which statements best describe your behavior. For example, in section **1** you might allocate 3 points to **b**, 3 points to **d**, and 4 points to **g**. You can distribute the points any way you like, even allocating 10 points to a single statement. Keep a note of your answers and see the opposite page for scoring and interpretation.

1. What I believe I can contribute to a team:
a. I sense what is workable in a familiar situation.
b. I can draw people out when I detect they have something of value to contribute.
c. I am ready to face personal unpopularity if it leads to worthwhile results in the end.
d. Producing ideas is one of my natural assets.
e. I can quickly spot new opportunities.
f. I can advance an unbiased case for alternative courses of action.
g. I work well with a wide range of people.
h. My capacity to follow through has much to do with my personal effectiveness.

2. When I am on a team my weak points are:
a. I am at ease only in well-structured and controlled meetings.
b. I am too generous toward those with any point of view to air, however irrelevant.
c. I am sometimes perceived as too forceful and authoritarian.
d. I get caught up in my own ideas and lose track of the general drift.
e. I talk a lot once new ideas emerge.
f. My critical approach makes it difficult for me to join in enthusiastically with colleagues.
g. I find it difficult to lead from the front, because I am overresponsive to the feelings of the group.
h. I sometimes worry unnecessarily over detail.

3. When working with other people:
a. I ensure that all essential work is organized.
b. I can influence them without pressuring them.

c. I am ready to press for action to ensure that the meeting does not lose sight of its objective.
d. I always contribute something original.
e. I look for the latest in new developments.
f. My cool judgment is widely appreciated.
g. I am always ready to back a good suggestion.
h. My vigilance minimizes careless mistakes.

4. What gives me satisfaction in a job is:
a. Finding practical solutions to problems.
b. Getting people to agree on necessary action.
c. Exerting a strong influence on decisions.
d. Stretching my imagination.
e. Meeting people with something new to offer.
f. Analyzing situations and weighing options.
g. Fostering good working relationships.
h. Giving a task my full attention.

5. If I were given a difficult task to complete in a limited time with unfamiliar colleagues:
a. I would feel like retiring to a corner to devise a way out of the impasse.
b. I would work with the most positive person, however difficult he or she might be.
c. I would try to discover from different individuals what they might best contribute.
d. My natural sense of urgency would help to ensure that we did not fall behind schedule.
e. I would keep cool and maintain my capacity to think straight.
f. I would remain purposeful under pressure.
g. I would take a lead if no progress occurred.
h. I would open up discussions to stimulate new thoughts and to get something moving.

6. In dealing with problems:
a. I cannot get started without clear goals.
b. I am conscious of demanding things from others that I cannot do myself.
c. I am impatient with those who obstruct progress.
d. I sometimes cannot explain complex points.
e. I tend to get bored easily and rely on others to get me going.
f. Others criticize me for being too analytical.
g. I hesitate to pursue my views when opposed.
h. My perfectionism can hold up proceedings.

Combined talents
*Successful problem-solving teams are those
made up of a variety of personalities, each
contributing different abilities and attitudes.*

How do you score?

Each letter **a** to **h** stands for a type of team role. To find
out which roles suit you best, add up the points that you
allocated to **a** statements; then count all the points you
have given to **b**s, **c**s, and so on.

Interpreting your scores

a stands for Company Worker, **b** for Chairperson, **c** for
Shaper, **d** for Idea Maker, **e** for Resource Investigator, **f**
for Monitor-Evaluator, **g** for Team Worker, and **h** for
Completer-Finisher. Most people will find their scores
divided among several of these roles.

Your highest scores show the ways in which you
contribute most effectively to a group. Your lowest
scores denote roles to which you are largely unsuited. In
an ideal team situation, you would have attributes that
other team members did not possess; conversely, your
weaker areas would be compensated for by other
members of the group.

• **Company Worker:** A highly conscientious worker
committed to company goals. Self-controlled, tough-
minded, trusting, tolerant, calm. Lacks original ideas,
however, and tends to be inflexible.

• **Chairperson:** A natural manager of people, receptive
to the views of others, but strong enough to reject their
ideas if necessary. Calm, realistic, self-disciplined, able
to pull the team together.

• **Shaper:** An extroverted leader, more aggressive and
impatient than the Chairperson. Can be argumentative
and disagreeable, but also good-humored and resilient

in the face of opposition. Can galvanize a stagnant
group or disrupt a well-functioning one.

• **Idea Maker:** A highly intelligent and creative
individual who produces original ideas. Dominant,
imaginative, tender-minded, radical. Often seen as
an oddball or loner. Needs leeway to contribute
skills, but also needs to be kept under control.

• **Resource Investigator:** An enthusiastic
extrovert who takes up and develops others' ideas.
Of average intelligence, versatile, sociable,
enthusiastic, and relaxed. Adept at exploring
available resources and naturally managerial.

• **Monitor-Evaluator:** A serious-minded
individual with sound, impartial judgment. Prudent
and careful, a decision-maker who can mean the
difference between company failure and success.

• **Team Worker:** A sensitive communicator who
fosters team spirit. Diplomatic, perceptive, trusting,
sensitive, sociable. Makes a popular manager.

• **Completer-Finisher:** A self-disciplined and
thorough person capable of seeing matters through
to a conclusion. Perfectionist, hard-working, steady,
pays scrupulous attention to detail and always
finishes a job off. Prone to anxiety and, though seen
as calm, often susceptible to physical stress.

CHAPTER FIVE

CREATIVITY FOR LIFE

THE PURSUIT OF CREATIVITY is not just a pastime for vacations, weekends, or occasional leisure hours. It should be an integral part of your daily existence. By adopting a more imaginative attitude to all your spheres of activity, it is possible to sow the seeds of originality in almost any endeavor that you might choose to undertake.

Inevitably, as individuals age and gain experience of life, they lose some of the natural creativity that most children possess. But seeing the world in narrow, predetermined patterns need not be an inevitable consequence of growing older. You can respond positively to change and keep a childlike freshness in everything you do, no matter how old or young you may be.

By observing a child at play you can learn much about basic creative principles such as risktaking and the benefits of disorder and chaos. This chapter opens with an examination of the nature of creativity in childhood, and offers a selection of simple and entertaining tests and games that will help even small children to explore the range of their imaginative potential and demonstrate their inventiveness.

Trying new hobbies or learning new skills is an essential feature of being creative. Not only does a new project keep your mental faculties sharp by keeping them stimulated, it also enables you to broaden your skills. This chapter will give you an opportunity to consider which of the various creative outlets you might be good at, in part by looking at the types of activities that appealed to you in the past. There are also three mini-workshops in design, creative writing, and caricature, so that you can sample these areas and decide whether you wish to pursue them farther.

Creativity, of course, cannot be programmed. But a section of handy hints and tips will remind you of the importance of gradual progression from small creative efforts to larger ones.

Finally, remember that you have the potential to be as creative as anyone else. If you nurture the urge to bring imagination to everything you do, you will find enormous reward in the effort.

UNLIKE A PLANT THAT GIVES ONLY ONE VARIETY OF FRUIT, THE CREATIVE IMAGINATION PRODUCES FRESH GROWTH IN EVERY SHAPE AND COLOR.

CREATIVE PARENTING

CHILDREN ARE NATURALLY INVENTIVE, so they do not have to be taught to be creative. They believe everything is possible, perhaps because they have so little experience of life. Unconstrained by fixed perceptions of the world, their minds have not yet settled into predictable patterns.

This state of innocence leaves children free to make unusual connections and come up with fresh, original ideas. Their abundant creativity reveals itself in endless games of make-believe, as well as in the pictures they paint and the stories they make up. Unfortunately, this natural talent often vanishes by adulthood, suppressed by the demands for conformity that are imposed on children by their parents, schools, and society.

Confidence boosters

Psychologists have identified a number of ways that parents can help their children resist this tendency and preserve their creativity. Parents can, for example, encourage their children to become independent and confident enough to make their own decisions. This is more difficult than it sounds. As Austrian psychologist Otto Rank has pointed out, parents feel responsible for what happens to their children, so their natural instinct is to maintain control rather than run the risk of watching their offspring endanger themselves in some way.

In order to develop a sufficient degree of self-confidence, children need to feel that their parents support them no matter what choices they make. This is not to say, of course, that you should encourage children to take silly risks, only that you must choose your moments carefully. You might think twice, for example, before criticizing a child who proclaims that wearing a neon orange shirt with purple pants is the epitome of fashion.

Parents who foster creativity in their children do so not only by giving them freedom, but also by collaborating in their pursuits. The parents of American filmmaker Steven Spielberg, for example,

WORLDS APART

Apart from environmental influences, biological factors may contribute to the loss of creativity as a child ages. A youngster's brain has many more nerve cells, or neurons, than does an adult brain. In a process called pruning that begins during infancy, many of these extra neurons die each day, while others settle into patterns that will be retained permanently. One theory asserts that this makes some loss of creativity inevitable during childhood. But other research maintains that, since the neural pathways laid down in childhood survive into later life, good thinking habits established early on may make a direct contribution to adult creativity.

Research has also shown that children's brain-wave patterns are different from those of adults. Even when children are fully awake, their brains are abundant with the slow theta waves that, in adults, occur primarily during the dreamlike period just before sleep (see page 38). Such brainwave patterns may be what enables children to lose themselves in fantasy. As they grow older, however, the theta waves begin to fade, taking with them the flair for make-believe.

The power of make-believe

For the limitless imagination of a child, the boundaries of reality and fantasy are never clearly defined. A simple toy can readily become a springboard to a whole different reality.

HOW CREATIVE IS YOUR CHILD?

This exercise is designed to bring out your child's skill at creating images, using simple shapes as building blocks. The five shapes that can be used are shown below. Your child may make them as small or as large as required, and any of the shapes may be used as often as he or she likes.

To carry out the exercise, encourage your child to rearrange the shapes to represent cars, dogs, flowers, and other simple everyday objects. Suggest that the child also draw different versions of the same objects. This test can be performed in many different ways; there are no wrong answers.

The level of creativity will reveal itself in the fluency with which your child generates images and in the range of uses he or she finds for each of the shapes. Below are examples of possible results.

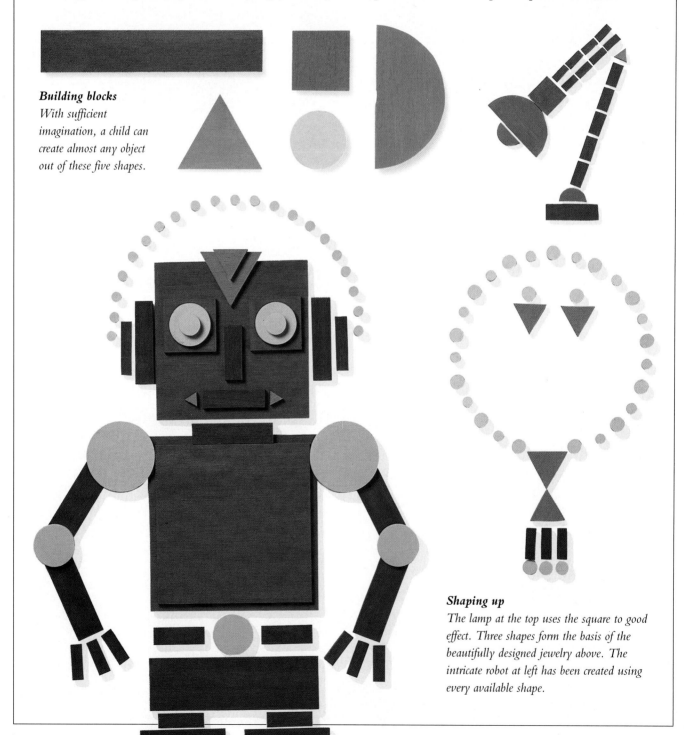

Building blocks
With sufficient imagination, a child can create almost any object out of these five shapes.

Shaping up
The lamp at the top uses the square to good effect. Three shapes form the basis of the beautifully designed jewelry above. The intricate robot at left has been created using every available shape.

ASK-AND-GUESS

Have fun exploring your child's imagination with this creative exercise. Ask him or her to study carefully the picture below, then describe or write down exactly what is happening. Next, ask the child to speculate about why this action might be taking place—what has happened previously to cause this situation. The more ideas that are produced, the better. Finally, encourage the youngster to imagine several ways in which the story might end.

Older children can be given a time limit of five minutes for each stage. Turn to page 141 for a selection of possible answers.

discussed his ideas with him when he was a boy and found ways to allow him to try them out. With their support he managed to become—at 21—the youngest film director in Hollywood.

Parental involvement

Appointed family photographer by his father at an early age, Spielberg began to make short movies with an 8-mm camera. These projects were more than mere recordings of birthday and Thanksgiving celebrations; they were stories on film with pre-ordained plots and characters. Spielberg's sisters usually had starring roles and his mother assisted him on his first production—a horror movie—by cooking 30 cans of cherries to serve as simulated blood. Of course, not all parents produce a young

Steven Spielberg. But anyone raising a child can learn from his story. Spielberg's parents encouraged him to follow *his* interests, not theirs, and thus avoided a common failing of parents—that of pushing their children to achieve things that they themselves have failed to accomplish.

A mother, for example, who arranges dance lessons for her daughter may do so because ballet was something she longed to study. The mother may be ignoring her daughter's own talents, which very well might reside elsewhere.

Freedom to imagine

Most young children have the ability to turn household items into fanciful playthings. A blanket, for example, can become a flying carpet, a tent, or

Improving on nature
Ask your child to draw ways of improving the human body. Four ideas are pictured at right—a long neck to see over crowds, four arms for doing homework and playing games at the same time, a second mouth for eating extra food, and a propeller to fly to school with. Then ask the child to improve a bicycle or a pair of shoes in the same way.

an ocean on which to set sail in a cardboard box. Parents can take steps to ensure that this ability to see grand possibilities in even the plainest of objects does not fade away entirely as a child grows older.

One practical step is to provide children with simple objects for play—such as wooden blocks, pieces of material, stones, or even vegetables—rather than always supplying single-purpose toys. Psychologists Scott G. Isaksen and Donald J. Treffinger also suggest stimulating a child's imagination with what they call "idea-starters." Simply take an opening phrase, such as, "If I could do anything, I would...," or "Why don't we...," and

encourage your child to finish it (either orally or in writing). Try to play this game with a young child at least once or twice a week.

Game of perception
Another way to enhance a child's perceptions is to play the "know-your-fruit" game. Each child is given a different piece of the same kind of fruit—oranges, for example—and asked to study its size, shape, and distinguishing features. All the fruit is then placed in a bag, and each child has to reach in and find his or her own fruit simply by feel. (Older children could perhaps be asked to describe what

made the fruit recognizable.) By the end of the game, the children will no longer think all pieces of fruit are the same; they will appreciate the subtle individuality of each one and consequently be more aware of differences in the world around them. Try to invent similar games to stimulate the other senses—sight, hearing, and smell.

Flexible attitudes

Parents can also help their children become more creative by encouraging them to develop a flexible attitude toward problem solving. If your child is having difficulty with one area of school work, for example, help him or her think of ways to make the troublesome subject more interesting. A child who dislikes story writing, for example, could be encouraged to draw a picture that tells the story before putting it down in words.

Above all, cultivate a positive attitude toward hard work; children should learn that reward is contingent on effort. Do remember, though, that children need to be allowed to explore the world at their own pace and should not have unnecessary time limitations placed on their play.

With this kind of leeway and support, children are able to enter the "flow" stage of creativity, in which time does not matter and concentration is at its peak, more naturally than adults. In this respect, as the English poet William Wordsworth wrote, "the child is father of the man."

LEARN TO PLAY

Just as an adult might be a professional doctor, sales person, or homemaker, children are professional players. Their job is to entertain themselves all day long, using originality and fantasy to create different worlds. By watching children do this job, adults can learn much about creativity, lessons they can then apply to their own lives. Here are some pointers on how children operate:

• Children are messy. Chaos often provides more possibilities and fun than living in a world that is tidy and regimented.

• Children take risks. They have wild, funny, and silly ideas because they are not concerned with coming up with the "right" answers.

• Children show perseverance and inventiveness. They can play with an object for weeks on end, never feeling restricted by its intended function.

• Children are open to new information. They tend, moreover, to take in new ideas without instantly judging or categorizing them.

• Children have endless time. They stay with an activity as long as it holds their imagination.

• Children are not restricted by knowledge of the real world. They are open to all possibilities.

CREATIVE AT WHAT?

MOST PEOPLE APPLY THEIR creative instincts chiefly toward the goal of enlivening their daily routine, both at home and work. But if you wish to engage in a more sustained form of creative activity, you will need to focus your efforts on a particular area.

Of course, some people are in the fortunate position of knowing in their bones where to direct their energies. Others, however, don't know where to begin. They may have a vague idea that they would like to follow one or more creative pursuits, but they don't know how to proceed from there or even how to narrow down the choices.

Get rid of old labels
You could choose an activity for which you showed some aptitude early in life; however, you might do better to free yourself of old—and perhaps outdated—evaluations of your abilities and talents. Although past teachers may have once labeled you "musical," "artistic," or "numerate," such assessments may not hold true any longer.

Upon further reflection, you may also recognize that pressure from your peers, parental expectations, the influence of a particular teacher, or just plain shyness kept you away from certain pursuits during high school or college. It is quite possible for someone who never sang in a choir or played a musical instrument to become a proficient musician, or for someone who never painted when young to become an accomplished artist.

Undiscovered talents
Your most promising area for development may not be obvious, however. The pages that follow provide a structured way to make an initial assessment of your suitability for different types of creative activity. Begin by trying the general self-assessment exercise at right, which aims to help you reassess skills and activities you may have tried in the past.

Then try the design, writing, and drawing workshops on pages 126 to 129 to see if you have any hidden talents in those particular endeavors. Remember, your chosen pursuit should be one that you clearly enjoy, rather than one you think you ought to enjoy. Now is the time to follow your heart's desires.

FOCUS ON YOUR ACHIEVEMENTS

In his best-selling career guide *What Color Is Your Parachute?*, Richard Nelson Bolles offers an original and effective method for assessing your general job skills. You can easily adapt his technique to assess your creative potential as well.

Bolles recommends setting aside a few hours to think about occasions in your life when you accomplished something positive. Perhaps you won an academic prize while in high school, or successfully completed a home improvement project, or organized an effective campaign to prevent a highway from being built through a local wildlife reserve. It does not matter whether the accomplishments were achieved during childhood or adult life, nor whether they fell during working or leisure hours.

Narrow down your remembrances to three specific occasions, then write down what happened in each case. Three paragraphs will do for each account. You may end up with something like the sample story "Sporting Chance" opposite.

Skilful listing
Once you have completed your stories, you can use them to analyze your areas of highest creative potential. Look at the stories carefully and list the skills or qualities that you exhibited, and any other relevant aspect of the episode. This list will provide pointers that you can follow.

Take Stephen, for example. Here was a boy much admired for his skill in painting model soldiers. He wanted to take up a new hobby as an adult, but wasn't sure where his strengths lay. By analyzing the skills he had employed in his painting, and remembering the intrinsic qualities of the pastime he had enjoyed, he was able to make the following list: indoors, solitary, attention to detail, accurate application, patience, and visible end product.

After considering the classes available at his local evening school, and matching them up with his list, he discovered—rather to his surprise—that a course in jewelry making suited his needs.

SPORTING CHANCE

This tale dates back to a time when the author, a male, was still in high school.

"In my early teens, I used to go fishing. It was while fishing that I started to jump from one side of the stream to the other. The distance I jumped increased as I became more proficient, and I always made a point of jumping over deep water so that if I didn't make the other side, the water would break my fall. I got wet on quite a few occasions.

"However, when the final field day at high school arrived, I was able to put all this practice to good use. I had entered the long jump, and as I ran up to the takeoff line, I imagined the sand in the landing area to be the stream. I jumped farther than I ever had before and captured first place, breaking the school record. One sport had helped me succeed in another."

By recalling this episode, the author was reminded that he was gifted with better-than-average physical coordination and that he liked activities in which he was something of a pioneer. If his other stories showed similar characteristics, he might conclude that he could prove inventive in experimental modern dance.

DESIGN A DINER

Imagine that you were asked to present some ideas for a high-concept diner called Bronto's, designed loosely around a theme of prehistoric life. You might come up with some ideas similar to those shown at right.

Now try the same exercise for a wholly different style of eatery—one based on the fashions and events of the 1960s. You have to suggest how the restaurant's name and logo, its decor, the outfits of the waiters and waitresses, the menu design, and so on can contribute to the desired effect. You don't necessarily have to be able to draw to perform this exercise—you can describe your ideas in words— but it will help if you can at least produce some sketches, however rough.

Practical interpretation

Start out by writing down the key ideas that the 1960s bring to mind: The Beatles, James Bond, the Twist, Kennedy, Pop Art, the miniskirt, Martin Luther King Jr., long hair, world peace, flower power, the moon landing, Woodstock, kaftans, and so on. Then work out how such ideas might be brought into play in the restaurant.

What design could you use for the uniforms— astronauts' spacesuits perhaps? Could menu items tie in with the theme—how about Beatleburgers? Consider an overall decor and color scheme—a psychedelic style, perhaps, with a "freaky" light show. Dreaming up the restaurant's name and logo will probably be the most difficult task, so you may wish to leave that for last.

If you find you are quite good at this exercise, you might do well to become involved in some design-oriented activity—for instance, interior decor, fashion or poster design.

Eating out at Bronto's
A prehistoric theme has been applied to a downtown diner with amusing results. Try to create your own design with the same elements: a logo, cutlery, food and drinks with clever names, and so on.

Imitation elegance
Dining tables and chairs made out of fake stone slabs could be complemented with bone candlesticks for cozy evening meals in the "cave."

Close to the bone
Knives, forks, and spoons have imitation bone handles to reinforce the caveman theme.

Drink rocktails
Cocktails are served in plastic glasses that are made to look like horn. Plastic baby dinosaurs' heads on sticks substitute for more conventional cocktail stirrers.

Diner delights
"Dinosaurs" serve T Rex cave-cooked steaks, prepared "well done," "medium rare," or "extinct," with stone cut French fries and Bronto broccoli, or a Hunter-gatherer side salad.

Picture the name
The logo is a friendly brontosaurus nestling on top of the diner's name.

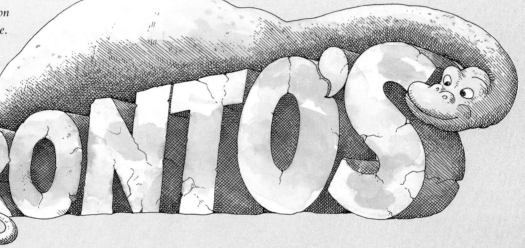

Solid menu
Constructed from plastic to resemble stone slabs, the menus of food and beverage offerings have printing that appears to be chipped out of the granite.

Behind the mask
An optional Triceratops mask keeps the kids out of trouble while their parents enjoy their meal.

127

TELL A TALE

Many people cringe at the idea of putting pen to paper. Like all spheres of creative activity, however, you won't know if you have a talent for writing unless you give it a try. The two picture stories below make a good starting point for evaluating your literary talents. Of the two drawings in each set, the picture at left depicts the beginning of a story and the picture at right its conclusion.

Choose the picture sequence that most captures your imagination and make up a short story that links the two scenes. To come up with a coherent tale, you will need to imagine a sequence of events that move from the one to the other. For example, in "A watery end?" you might begin by asking yourself who is making the shadow that upsets the dog. Then imagine a sequence of events that ends with someone—or something—overboard.

If you have trouble getting started, it may help to use brainstorming techniques (see pages 102 to 107) when looking at the pictures to generate as

A WATERY END?

STAYING IN TOUCH

many ideas as possible. Remember that a short story needs characters, a setting, some kind of action and, frequently, dialogue. How you treat these elements is up to you. Don't be satisfied with simply describing external events; creative writing embraces the inner world—the thoughts and emotions of the characters—as well as the outer one. Give yourself at least an hour for writing, then examine the story's structure and your writing style.

Evaluate your writing

Look critically at the characters, setting, and plot of your story. Ask yourself such questions as: Do all the characters contribute to the tale? Is there enough action to hold a reader's attention? Does the dialogue reflect the way people really speak? (To develop a feel for dialogue, start listening to the cadence and content of people's conversations.)

Now focus on the writing style. One way of giving the text depth and richness is to avoid relying solely on your sense of sight; include descriptions based on all of the senses—smell, touch, taste, and hearing. Also try to avoid trite phrases, such as "snow-clad slopes," that have been used many times before. Although your phrases and metaphors should be fresh, the words themselves should be familiar. Use simple phrases rather than roundabout descriptions, and don't use a long word where a short one will do.

But style considerations aside, the best advice to a would-be writer is to write from personal experience. Your story will be much better for it.

A COMIC TOUCH

Satirical caricatures have amused the readers of newspapers and magazines for hundreds of years. But you don't have to be exceptionally good at drawing to be able to create caricatures that exaggerate people's characteristics. If you have ever doodled, you can caricature.

The key to this art form is to exaggerate the truth and to reduce a face to a few startling features: a heavy brow, for example, or a pair of monster lips. Caricature frequently also encapsulates the subject's mood or character by including a prop or emphasizing a gesture. With just a few quick lines it should be possible to sum up a person's face, their physical features and their character.

Study Eliot's face above and think how you might have drawn his caricature. Below are one cartoonist's interpretations of this face.

Now try your hand at some caricatures of your own face after studying it in a mirror, then progress to drawings of friends from photographs. It will help if you draw each feature with just a few strokes of the pencil. If you enjoy this form of creativity, it won't be long before you progress to the art of cartooning and drawing whole scenes to humorous effect.

Pulling out features
Eliot's face is studied intently as the scale of exaggeration increases from left to right. First his hair is given prominence; then his nose and chin come under scrutiny, becoming larger and more pronounced as the caricature develops.

A PROGRAM FOR CREATIVITY

KNOWING HOW TO BE more creative is only the beginning; you must now put your newfound skills and understanding into daily practice. As with all self-improvement programs, it is up to you to make a conscious and sustained effort.

One line of approach is to develop specific interests or projects that will tap your creative skills. You can select from an almost limitless range of possibilities—from painting to pottery, from macramé to music, from carpentry to choreography.

Choose something you really enjoy and throw yourself into it with wholehearted enthusiasm. Sign up for courses in your special interest, read books on the subject, and make it the focus of your vacations. Build friendships with people who share the same enthusiasm. A creative outlet can enrich your life over many years and give you a place to channel your energies in retirement.

Cultivate new habits

You can be creative in many different ways, not just in one or two narrow areas. The effort to be more original should become an ingrained habit, something you do at all times and in all parts of your life. It need not be something that is reserved only for special occasions.

Take the simple example of greeting cards. Everyone sends them, but very few people see them as a challenge to their creativity. Yet every time you want to contact someone, you have a chance to be inventive and to make it a more individual gesture. If you are sending a store-bought card, you can devote a little extra effort to the message you write inside, making up a rhyme or a joke for the occasion. Or you could add a little drawing of your own—a caricature or some affectionate image.

If you have more time, you can also make your own greeting cards. These can range from the simplest effort—a photo stuck to the front of a folded piece of construction paper—to quite elaborate creations involving drawing, painting, collage, or other artistic techniques. The same degree of imagination can be applied in assembling your wardrobe. Start, perhaps, by personalizing store-bought accessories, then move on to making some

of your own clothes. Similarly, you could progress from planting decorative borders to creating an exotic or scented garden. The amount of time you devote to such activities will depend, of course, on how much importance you give them. By demanding more of yourself and your imagination, you will encourage your creativity and inventiveness to blossom and grow. Monitor your day-to-day routine to see where an injection of originality may be needed. Of course, you may not want to innovate and improvise all the time—habit and routine do have their place in life. But avoid letting any side of your existence become excessively dull and repetitive. You have a chance to be more inventive every time you cook a meal, for example, or carry out home improvements.

Look also at the creative possibilities of your workplace. Make a list of working methods that stimulate and develop your creativity; keep a separate list for practices that discourage innovation. Then decide how and where to make changes.

The personal touch

A sprinkling of creative thinking in your personal life may improve relations with your nearest and dearest. Apply creative thinking techniques to obstacles you need to overcome in your relationships. If your emotional life is stuck in a rut, try using creative thinking to come up with new methods of approaching old problems. By being open and flexible, you may find a way to put a new slant on things.

Fortunately, creativity has an inner momentum; the more creative activities you attempt, the more opportunities for creativity you will find opening up. For example, a new outdoor activity such as hiking might encourage you to develop an interest in sketching, which in turn may lead you to explore botany and geology. The joy and excitement of creativity often lie in the journey itself, and not necessarily in arriving at a destination.

Everyday invention
You can develop creativity at work, on vacation, or at home, in areas that range from present giving and household improvement to sports and personal relationships.

FRAMES OF MIND

Review this checklist whenever you feel that you are losing your creative edge. Each frame contains a useful hint that will help you overcome a particular problem, or broaden your creative perspective.

Don't stay stuck
Always question the techniques you use for problem solving. Are you so stuck in a rut that you cannot work out problems creatively? Try different ways to solve the problem—simplifying it, for example.

Time it right
Make better use of your time. Identify the wasted hours in your day that could be devoted to creative tasks. Cut out mindless activities that dilute your resolve and deaden your imagination.

Study skills
Enroll in a course to build skills in your chosen area. Read books and magazines on the subject.

Have a hunch
Learn to rely on your intuition. It might be right, it might be wrong, but it is worth taking notice every time you have a gut feeling about an idea.

Relax your mind
Learn to induce alpha-wave thinking using relaxation techniques such as yoga. Make the most of all the ways in which your mind works; for example, begin taking note of your dreams when you wake up.

Take the challenge
Strive to find solutions to every problem you come up against. Treat difficulties as creative challenges rather than as burdens to avoid.

Flex your thinking
Practice mental flexibility. Never be satisfied with the way you have always done things. There may be a better option available.

Be curious
Be as curious as you can about everything around you. Get into the habit of asking questions. If you feel embarrassed because you don't understand something, remember that the more you ask, the more you will know.

Keep going
Try to maintain your perseverance and productivity when the going gets tough. In the end, your creativity will be increased.

Look more closely
Open your eyes to the world around you. See everything in as much detail as you can—and, ideally, in new ways. Instead of always watching the world at eye level try looking up at buildings and down at the ground. Appreciate the beauty of things as simple as the pattern formed by drops of rain on a leaf.

Take a chance
If you cannot think of a subject for a creative project or despair in solving a problem, try out a few random-thinking techniques. Be open to the element of serendipity in your life.

Build up contacts
Contact organizations of people with creative interests similar to your own. Seek out individuals who can respond knowledgeably to your projects.

Think visually
If you are a person who habitually relies solely on words, try making your thoughts visual instead of verbal. Externalizing problems by drawing matrices or other pictorializing devices can speed up your problem solving as well.

Dare to be different
Don't worry too much if your creative plans seem a bit wacky. Ideas that are out of the ordinary are often the most creative. But learn to recognize and discard ideas that have no merit.

Dig deep
If you have a special interest, research it as thoroughly as you can. You can never know too much, and no piece of knowledge is ever totally irrelevant.

Make a space
Find a suitable place in which to work on your projects and allocate time in your schedule. By focusing daily effort on a project, you can make it a part of your life.

SOLUTIONS

Page 8:
Ways with words
If you provided more than six alternatives to each word, you are already highly creative in your verbal skills; if you had trouble thinking up more than two synonyms for each word, consult these lists for suggestions about words you may have overlooked.

HOT: fiery, burning, up-to-the-minute, bright, lucky, exciting, aroused, radioactive, spicy, sexy, stolen

SOFT: yielding, undemanding, malleable, easy, gentle, subtle, liberal, sensitive, sluggish, silky, quiet

SIMPLE: uncomplicated, basic, rudimentary, naive, easy, unintelligent, unadorned

YOUNG: undeveloped, immature, childish, inexperienced, fresh, new, growing, tender

COOL: cold, frigid, calm, autumnal, nonchalant, unemotional, controlled, nonresponsive

TOUGH: hard, chewy, unruly, resilient, glutinous, ruthless, unfeeling, excellent, difficult

Page 9:
Meet your match
1. This is the correct solution to the "six equal triangles" problem.

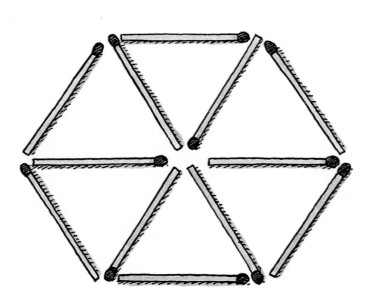

2. Below (A) shows one way to make four squares by moving three matches; the second solution (B) has a twist—you make a square within a square by moving only two matches.

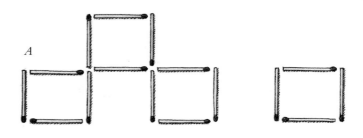

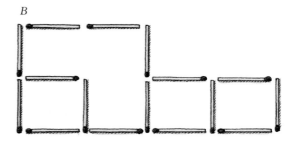

3. Here are two simple solutions to the puzzle.

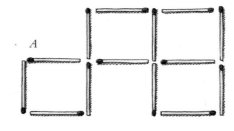

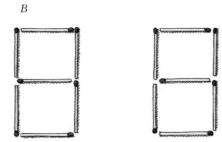

4. This is the most difficult of the matchstick problems. The answer is to assemble the matchsticks into a three-dimensional shape, as shown below.

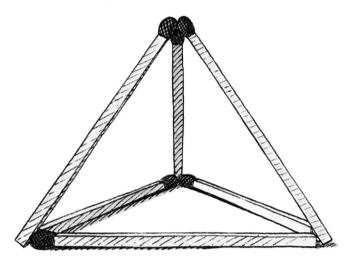

Page 10:
Brave new world
Here are some suggestions of what a three-legged world might be like:
- You could run and swim much faster.
- Bathtubs, beds, and chairs would need to be wider.
- Painting your toenails would take a lot longer.
- Riding a motorcycle would be very difficult.
- You could rest one leg at a time while walking.
- Ballet would look completely different.
- You might trip more often.
- Crossing your legs would involve more decisions.

You may have thought of others. Any changes to buildings, vehicles, tools, or activities that would be necessary to accommodate three-legged people are valid.

Page 11:
Picture this
Both pictures have been designed to be open-ended and invite almost any response. Here are two sample stories:

Left-hand picture: Tom runs his own small floristry business. After many years of experimenting, he has at last developed an extraordinary variety of rose with a beautiful scent. Tom is trying hard to market his rose and he keeps samples of the blooms in various plastic bags in a sample case. After returning from lunch, he discovers that an unscrupulous competitor has not only destroyed all the plants in his greenhouse, but has also

thrown a brick through the window of his office. Tom holds his head in his hands in despair.

Right-hand picture: Grant is a professional baseball player. He has just arrived home from an awards ceremony where he was presented with an inscribed bat for his charity work. Because his wife had not attended the ceremony, claiming she felt ill, Grant had left early, eager to show her the award. On his return, however, he finds her at home with another man. Overcome with anger at her deception and her indifference to his feelings, he clenches the bat tightly, fighting the impulse to use it as a weapon.

Page 18:
Star gazing
Four five-pointed star shapes are highlighted here.

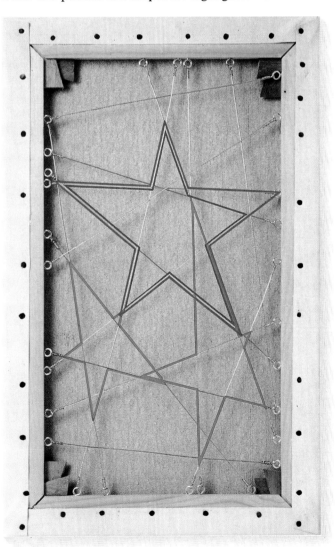

Page 19:
Hide and seek

At first, the two canvases look as if they depict nothing more than random shapes. But once you discover the bearded man and the cow, as shown below, you may find it difficult to see the meaningless patterns you saw before.

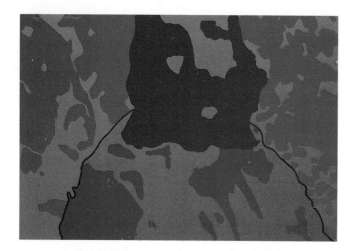

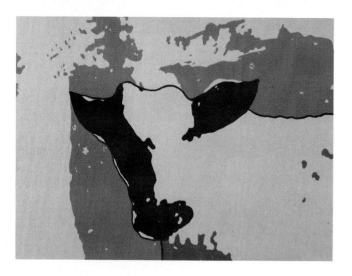

Page 44:
The hidden number puzzle

The correct answer is:

A (**9**) D (**1**)
D (**1**) U (**0**)
D (1) U (0) D (1)

You may have already worked out that U equals 0, because when D is added to U, D remains unchanged.

Next, deduce the value of D by looking at the fact that A plus D equals a two-digit number whose first digit is D. From this, D must be 1. (If a one-digit number is added to another one-digit number to total a two-digit number, that total must be between 10 and 18, so D must be 1). Replace the Us with 0s and Ds with 1s and you can work out the value of A: If 1+A=10, then A=9.

Page 46:
Break the chain

Only **four** links need to be cut—one single link, a string of two links, a string of four, and a string of eight.
The exchange of links goes like this:
On the first day, Dan gives the hotel manager one link; on the second he takes back the single link and gives the manager a string of two. On the third day, Dan gives the manager the one link again to add to his string of two; on the fourth, Dan takes back the two links and the one link, then gives the manager a string of four links. On the fifth day, Dan gives the manager the one link again to add to his four. The same pattern continues for the rest of the 15 days. This is the final breakdown of the links the hotel manager holds each day:

Day 1:	1 (single link)
Day 2:	2 (string of two)
Day 3:	2+1
Day 4:	4 (string of four)
Day 5:	4+1
Day 6:	4+2
Day 7:	4+2+1
Day 8:	8 (string of eight)
Day 9:	8+1
Day 10:	8+2
Day 11:	8+2+1
Day 12:	8+4
Day 13:	8+4+1
Day 14:	8+4+2
Day 15:	8+4+2+1

Page 48:
The towers of Hanoi
Below are the 15 moves you will need to make in order to solve the four-ring problem.

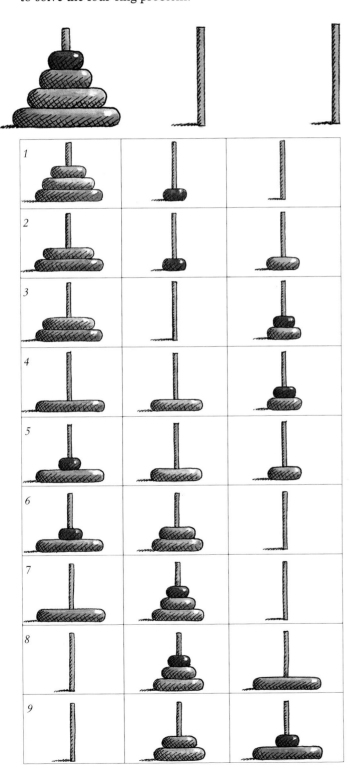

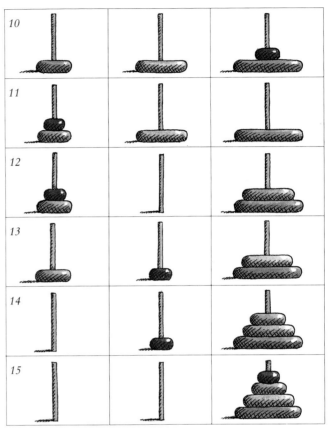

Page 49:
Counterfeit gold
To solve the simpler version with the three stacks of three coins, you can calculate the bad stack of coins by taking one coin from stack 1, two coins from stack 2, and all three coins from stack 3. If all the coins were good, these six coins should weigh 12 ounces. The number of ounces less than 12 gives the number of the stack with the counterfeit coins. For example, if the six coins weigh nine ounces, then the third pile was the counterfeit pile because nine taken from 12 equals three.

The same principle applies to the 10 stacks of 10 gold pieces. Take one from stack 1, two from stack 2, and so on up to 10 from stack 10. If all the coins were good, these 55 coins should weigh 110 ounces. The number of ounces less than 110 would provide the number of the stack with the counterfeit coins in it. So if the sixth pile was counterfeit, the 55 coins would weigh 104 ounces.

Page 51:
Brainteasers
1. George and Mabel are goldfish. The window was left

open and the wind knocked the goldfish bowl off the table onto the floor, where it smashed.

2. The carrot, hat, and lump of coal are all that remain of a snowman after the snow has melted.

Page 53:
Retrieve the ball
Probably the most effective way of retrieving the ball is to pour the milk into the pipe, so that the ball will float to the top of the pipe. Other ideas include breaking the coat hanger and flattening the ends with the wrench to make large tweezers to retrieve the ball; or making a paste from milk-moistened breakfast cereal, and using it to stick the top of the ball to one end of the clothes line—the theory being that as the paste dried it would set like glue, allowing the ball to be fished out. The craziest solution offered for this problem, by someone with more imagination than practical sense, was to turn the room upside down!

Page 55:
Cube teaser
The secret of the cube's construction is that the dovetails visible on adjoining sides are opposite ends of two parallel bars, so that the two halves can slide apart.

Page 59:
Tie up the string
The most straightforward solution to the string problem involves using the scissors or the hammer as weights, rather than for performing their usual functions. Tie either of these two objects to one of the pieces of string. This creates a pendulum that you can set into a wide swinging motion. Then take hold of the other piece of string and catch the scissors or hammer as it swings toward you. You can then untie the scissors or hammer (without letting go of the string) and tie the two pieces of string together. The clothes peg serves no purpose, unless you use it to hold the two strings temporarily together while you untie the hammer or scissors.

Page 60:
Secret message
Here are three possible solutions to the problem of sending a message, although you may think of others:

1. Put the mirror on a flat surface, and use some of the matches to form the letters SOS. Then light the candle with another match and drip melted wax over the message. This will stick the matches to the mirror, which the guard can transport to your contact.

2. Light the candle and drip wax onto the mirror. Before it hardens, scratch the letters SOS (or the Morse code equivalent: ··· --- ···) in the soft wax with a matchstick.

3. Light the candle, hold the mirror over it until it is blackened by the smoke, then spell out SOS on the surface with a matchstick.

Page 61:
Join the dots
1. Four lines: Working within the square shape defined by the dots constrains your thinking. Forget the square and you will find the four-line solution shown below.

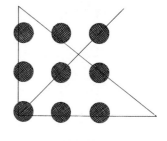

2. Three lines: If you get rid of the conceptual block that lines must run through the center of the dots, you can make a three-line solution.

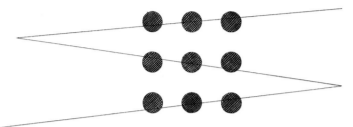

3. One line: A variety of ways exist for solving the nine dot test with one line. When you free your mind of all limitations the possibilities are endless. Here are a few variations: Put the paper with the nine dot problem on to the surface of a globe. Draw a single line twice round the globe, so that it goes through each set of dots.

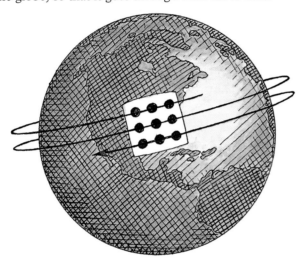

Or, draw very large dots on a piece of paper. Crumple up the paper and stab it with the pencil. By chance, you might manage to pierce all nine dots.

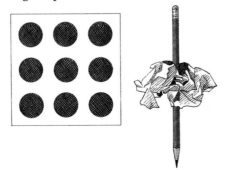

Another highly creative solution was proposed by a 10-year-old girl, who suggested drawing a line through all the dots with a very fat pen.

Page 61:
The water jar test
You can solve all the problems from 2 to 8 using the formula "B minus A minus 2C." Fill jar B, then use it to fill jar A once, and to fill jar C twice. This will leave the required amount of water in jar B.

Although this formula works for problems 7 and 8, however, there is a much simpler way of solving them: Just fill jar A and use it to fill jar C. This will leave the required amount in jar A. On average, only 25 percent of problem solvers spot this simpler solution.

Page 71:
Search for the symbol
Here are a few suggestions for corporate symbols:
Trucking company—elephant, camel, ant
Airline—arrow, butterfly, lark
Dry cleaner—penguin, snowflake, polar bear
Health club—greyhound, racehorse, dolphin

Page 73:
How tall?
Mary is **25 inches** tall and Jean is **35 inches** tall. Externalize the problem by drawing a line that shows Mary's height doubled. Next draw a line to represent Jean's height, which has to be bigger than Mary's height but smaller than that height doubled. You will then be able to "see" the answer.

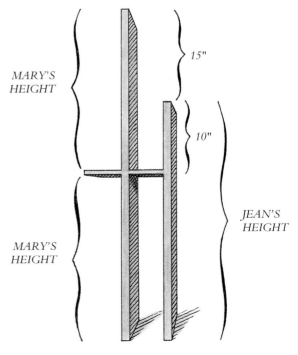

Page 74:
Musical instruments problem
This list tells who owns which instruments:

John	Bassoon and oboe
Guy	Oboe and trumpet
Steve	Clarinet and flute
Wayne	Trumpet and flute

Compare it with the list below, which puts the instruments in the order of their expense (with the most expensive one on top):

Most expensive

   Trumpet
   Flute
   Oboe
   Bassoon
   Clarinet

Least expensive

Looking at both lists, it immediately becomes apparent that Wayne has the most expensive instruments.

Page 74:
Marriage-go-round
By drawing a matrix and externalizing the problem, you are able to solve the puzzle. This is how you should have filled in your matrix step by step. (O symbolizes "married," X "not married"):

Statement 1: "Karen is Todd's sister and has three children." Put an "X" in the Todd/Karen square; since they are siblings, they cannot be married.

Statement 2: "Jim and his wife do not have children." Put an "X" in the Jim/Karen square, since you have just learned from statement 1 that Karen has three kids.

Statement 3: "Jim's wife has never met Julie, who is having an affair with Todd." Put an "X" in the Jim/Julie square, since Julie cannot be Jim's wife; put an "X" in the Todd/Julie square because they cannot be married if they are having an affair.

Statement 4: "Angela is so outraged by this that she is thinking of telling Todd's wife about it." Put an "X" in the Todd/Angela square, since they cannot be married. Todd's wife has to be Cathy, as she is the only one left. Fill in an "O" on the Todd/Cathy square, and an "X" on Cathy's other squares. With Cathy accounted for, the other married couple that emerges is Jim and Angela. Again fill in the relevant "O" and "Xs."

Statement 5: "Todd and David are twins." Put an "X" in the Karen/David square; they cannot be married, since you know that Karen is Todd's sister from

statement 1. She must also be David's sister, leaving Julie to be his wife. The only couple left is Karen and Peter. See below for a visual summary: Angela is married to Jim; Karen to Peter; Julie to David; Cathy to Todd.

	JIM	TODD	DAVID	PETER
ANGELA	O	X	X	X
KAREN	X	X	X	O
JULIE	X	X	O	X
CATHY	X	O	X	X

Page 75:
Test your visualization skills
1. Hole in the honeycomb
B is the piece that exactly fits in the hole.

140

2. Twisted whale

Here are the seven moves you need to make to arrive at the complete picture of the whale.

Starting point

4

1

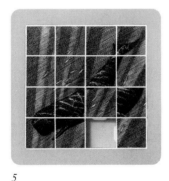

5

2

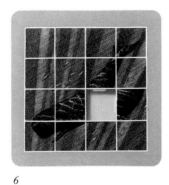

6

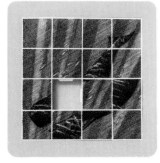

3

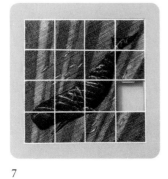

7

3. How many slices?

You get **14** pieces of melon.

The simplest way to visualize the number of pieces is to start with the red and blue cuts below. These obviously give you 4 pieces. Then imagine the green cut going clean across them: This must make 8 pieces. Now comes the most difficult move. The brown cut does not cross all the 8 pieces. In fact, it creates another 6 pieces, to give a total of 14.

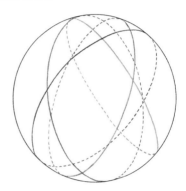

4. Malformations

Figure A: It is the only one that has two internal points at which three lines meet.

Page 121:
Ask-and-guess
Possible explanations for the action:

The boy did not want the goose to be slaughtered for Christmas, so he decided to steal it.

The goose lays golden eggs, so the woman stole it from the boy.

The boy took the goose because he needed some feathers to make a pillow for his sick father.

Possible outcomes of the action:

The goose flies away.

The woman trips and the boy escapes with the goose. Both of them run until they reach the edge of the world.

The number of stories a child invents indicates the degree of flexibility. The more unusual the answers, the freer he or she is from functional fixity.

INDEX

BIBLIOGRAPHY

James L. Adams, *The Care and Feeding of Ideas*; Addison-Wesley Publishing, Reading, MA, U.S., 1986

James L. Adams, *Conceptual Blockbusting*; Addison-Wesley Publishing, Reading, MA, U.S., 1990

Anne Anastasi, *Psychological Testing*; Macmillan Publishing Company, New York, NY, U.S., 1988

Rudolf Arnheim, *Visual Thinking*; University of California Press, Berkeley, CA, U.S., 1980

R. Meredith Belbin, *Management Teams: Why They Succeed or Fail*; Halstead Press, New York, NY, U.S., 1981

Margaret Boden, *The Creative Mind*; Basic Books, Crocker, MO, U.S., 1991

Richard Nelson Bolles, *What Color is Your Parachute?*; Ten Speed Press, Berkeley, CA, U.S., 1991

Edward de Bono, *Children Solve Problems*; Penguin Books, Harmondsworth, U.K., 1972

Edward de Bono, *De Bono's Thinking Course*; Facts on File, New York, NY, U.S., 1988

Edward de Bono, *Handbook for the Positive Revolution;* Penguin Books, Harmondsworth, U.K., 1991

Edward de Bono, *Serious Creativity*; HarperBusiness, New York, NY, U.S., 1992

Tony Buzan, *Make the Most of Your Mind*; S & S Trade, Kenmore, WA, U.S., 1986

Julia Casterton, *Creative Writing*; The Macmillan Press, Basingstoke, U.K., 1986

Ann Cushman, "Are You Creative?", *Utne Reader*, March/April 1992, pages 52-69

John S. Dacey, *Fundamentals of Creative Thinking*; Lexington Books, Lexington, MA, U.S., 1989

Ward Dean, M.D. and John Morgenthaler, *Smart Drugs and Nutrients*; B & J Publications, Santa Cruz, CA, U.S., 1991

Peter Evans and Geoff Deehan, *The Keys to Creativity*; Grafton Books, London, U.K., 1988

Henry Gleitman, *Basic Psychology*; W.W. Norton & Company, New York, NY, U.S., 1987

Daniel Goleman, "Pondering the Riddle of Creativity," *The New York Times*, March 22, 1992, page H1

Daniel Goleman, Paul Kaufman, and Michael Ray, *The Creative Spirit*; Dutton Books, New York, NY, U.S., 1991

"Intuition Quotient: A Test," *Omni*, April 1992, page 46

Arthur Koestler, *The Act of Creation*; Viking Penguin, New York, NY, U.S., 1990

Judith K. Larsen and Everitt M. Rogers, *Silicon Valley Fever*; Basic Books, Crocker, MO, U.S., 1984

Marvin Levine, *Effective Problem Solving*; Prentice Hall, Englewood Cliffs, NJ, U.S., 1988

Carol O. Madigan and Ann Elwood, *Brainstorms and Thunderbolts*; Macmillan Publishing Company, New York, NY, U.S., 1983

Albert Rothenberg, M.D., *Creativity and Madness*; The Johns Hopkins University Press, Baltimore, Maryland, U.S., 1990

Peter Russell and Roger Evans, *The Creative Manager;* Jossey-Bass Publishers, San Francisco, CA, U.S., 1992

Roger von Oech, *A Whack on the Side of the Head;* Warner Books, New York, NY, U.S., 1990

Robert W. Weisberg, *Creativity: Genius and Other Myths*; W.H. Freeman and Company, New York, NY, U.S., 1986

Thomas G. West, *In The Mind's Eye*; Prometheus Books, Buffalo, NY, U.S., 1991

CREDITS

Illustrators

Gail Armstrong, Debut Art, Paul Desmond, Phil Dobson, Nick Hardcastle, Ellis Nadler, Povl Webb

Modelmakers

Atlas Models, David Greenwood, Mike Shepherd

Photographers

Barbara Bellingham, Paul Bradforth, Simon Farnell, Mark Hamilton, Gary Kevin, Eitan Lee Al, Kevin Mallet, Alex Wilson.

Picture sources

The publishers are grateful to the following individuals and picture libraries for permission to reproduce their photographs.

The Image Bank **88-89** (background); **88** (center); **88** (center right); **88** (far right); **88-89** (center top); **89** (top left); **99** (below right); **132-33** (background)

Hulton Deutsch **73** (top right)

Pictures for Print **78-79** (all inset pictures)

*"All the really good ideas I ever had
came to me while I was milking a cow."*

Grant Wood